BOOKS BY KENNETH KOCH

Poems
Ko, or A Season on Earth
Permanently
Thank You and Other Poems
Bertha and Other Plays
When the Sun Tries to Go On
The Pleasures of Peace
Wishes, Lies and Dreams:
    Teaching Children to Write Poetry
A Change of Hearts:
    Plays, Films, and Other Dramatic Works
Rose, Where Did You Get That Red?
    Teaching Great Poetry to Children
The Art of Love
The Red Robins—a novel
The Duplications
I Never Told Anybody:
    Teaching Poetry Writing in a Nursing Home
Les Couleurs des Voyelles
The Red Robins—a play
The Burning Mystery of Anna in 1951
Sleeping on the Wing:
    An Anthology of Modern Poetry
    with Essays on Reading and Writing
    (with Kate Farrell)
Days and Nights
Selected Poems, 1950–1982

Selected Poems 1950–1982

Selected Poems 1950–1982

Kenneth Koch

Vintage Books
A Division of
Random House
New York

FIRST VINTAGE BOOKS EDITION, March 1985

Copyright © 1985 by Kenneth Koch

All rights reserved under International and Pan-American
Copyright Conventions. Published in the United States
by Random House, Inc., New York, and simultaneously in
Canada by Random House of Canada Limited, Toronto.
Hardcover edition published simultaneously by Random House, Inc.

*Grateful acknowledgment is made to the following for
permission to reprint previously published material:*

Grove Press, Inc.: Poems from *Thank You and Other Poems*,
by Kenneth Koch, Grove Press, Inc., 1962. Copyright © 1962 by
Kenneth Koch. Poems from *The Pleasures of Peace*, by Kenneth Koch,
Grove Press, Inc., 1969. Copyright © 1969 by Kenneth Koch. Reprinted
with permission of Grove Press, Inc.

Random House, Inc.: Poems from *The Art of Love*, by
Kenneth Koch. Copyright © 1972, 1974, 1975 by
Kenneth Koch. Poems from *Days and Nights*, by Kenneth Koch.
Copyright © 1982 by Kenneth Koch. Poems from
The Burning Mystery of Anna in 1951, by Kenneth Koch.
Copyright © 1977, 1978, 1979 by Kenneth Koch. Reprinted by
permission of Random House, Inc.

Jacket design by Katherine Koch

Front cover: Portrait of Kenneth Koch
by Fairfield Porter. Used by permission
of the Fairfield Porter Estate.

Library of Congress Cataloging in Publication Data

Koch, Kenneth.
Selected Poems, 1950–1982

I. Title.
PS3521.027A6   1985   811'.54   84–25824
ISBN 0–394–73771–7

Manufactured in the United States of America

Author's Note

These poems were written between 1950 and 1982 and published (in five collections) between 1962 and 1982. They are in roughly chronological order, except for a few poems in *The Pleasures of Peace* that were written, or a least begun, at the same time as those in *Thank You*. Two book-length narrative poems, *Ko, or A Season on Earth* and *The Duplications*, seemed to me better in their entirety than in excerpts and so are not included here; nor, for the same reason, is an earlier long poem called *When the Sun Tries to Go On*.

K. K.

1985

In memory of Janice

Contents

from

Thank You

On the Great Atlantic Rainway

I set forth one misted white day of June
Beneath the great Atlantic rainway, and heard:
"Honestly you smite worlds of truth, but
Lose your own trains of thought, like a pigeon.
Did you once ride in Kenneth's machine?"
"Yes, I rode there, an old man in shorts, blind,
Who had lost his way in the filling station; Kenneth was kind."
"Did he fill your motionless ears with resonance and stain?"
"No, he spoke not as a critic, but as a man."
"Tell me, what did he say?" "He said,
'My eyes are the white sky, the gravel on the groundway my sad
    lament.'"
"And yet he drives between the two. . . ." "Exactly, Jane,

And that is the modern idea of fittingness,
To, always in motion, lose nothing, although beneath the
Rainway they move in threes and twos completely
Ruined for themselves, like moving pictures."
"But how other?" "Formulalessness, to go from the sun
Into love's sweet disrepair. He would fondly express
'Rain trees'—which is not a poem, 'rain trees. . . .'"
"Still, it is mysterious to have an engine
That floats bouquets! and one day in the rear-vision
Mirror of his car we vowed delight,
The insufficiency of the silverware in the sunlight,
The dreams he steals from and smiles, losing gain."

"Yet always beneath the rainway unsyntactical
Beauty might leap up!" "That we might sing
From smiles' ravines, 'Rose, the reverse of everything,
May be profaned or talked at like a hat.'"
"Oh that was sweet and short, like the minuet
Of stars, which would permit us to seem our best friends
By silver's eminent lights! For nature is so small, ends
Falsely reign, distending the time we did
Behind our hope for body-work, riding with Kenneth."
Their voicing ceased, then started again, to complain
That we are offered nothing when it starts to rain
In the same way, though we are dying for the truth.

3

Summery Weather

One earring's smile
Near the drawer
And at night we gambling
At that night the yacht on Venice
Glorious too, oh my heavens
See how her blouse was starched up.
"The stars reminded me of youse."
"His lip sticks out. His eye is sailing.
I don't care what happens
Now," she says,
"After those winters in Florida!"
As for a pure dance
With oranges,
"All my factories
Need refilling,"
The corpse said, falling down between them.
"Okay okay
Here's a banana and a bandana
The light on a bright night,
With which, to finish, my personal challenge."
Oh how she admired him!
Lovely are fireworks;
Given, the shirts have a sale
To themselves; but
The wind is blowing, blowing!

The Brassiere Factory

Is the governor falling
From a great height?
Arm in arm we fled the brassiere factory,
The motion-boat stayed on the shore!
I saw how round its bottom was
As you walked into southern France—
Upon the light hair of an arm
Cigar bands lay!
I kissed you then. Oh is my bar
The insect of your will? The water rose,
But will the buffalo on
The nickel yet be still?
For how can windows hold out the light
In your eyes!
Darling, we fled the brassiere factory
In forty-eight states,
Arm in arm,
When human beings hung on us
And you had been arrested by the cloths
Were used in making, and I said, "The Goths
Know such delight," but still we fled, away
Into a dinner atmosphere
From all we knew, and fall asleep this day.
O maintenance men, with cruel eyes,
Then arm in arm we fled the listless factory!
The music changed your fingers' ends to pearl,
I punched you, you foolish girl,
For thanks to the metronome we got out alive, in the air
Where the sun filled us with cruelty!
There's what to do
Except despair, like pages! and laugh
Like prawns, about the sea!
Oh arm in arm we fled the industry
Into an earth of banks
And foolish tanks, for what bare breasts might be.

The Bricks

The bricks in a wall
Sang this song:
"We shall not fall
The whole day long
But white and small
Lie in abandon."

Then the fair maid
Passed with her love
And she to him said,
"There are stars above
Where they have been laid
Let us lie in abandon."

Then the wolf came
With his teeth in abandon
And the lion came
With his teeth in abandon
And they ravaged and he came
To the white stone

And he kissed the field's grass
And he lay in abandon.
"I forget if she was
Or he was the stone
Or if it was the animals,"
And, "Everything comes soon."

Desire for Spring

Calcium days, days when we feed our bones!
Iron days, which enrich our blood!
Saltwater days, which give us valuable iodine!
When will there be a perfectly ordinary spring day?
For my heart needs to be fed, not my urine
Or my brain, and I wish to leap to Pittsburgh
From Tuskegee, Indiana, if necessary, spreading like a flower
In the spring light, and growing like a silver stair.
Nothing else will satisfy me, not even death!
Not even broken life insurance policies, cancer, loss of health,
Ruined furniture, prostate disease, headaches, melancholia,
No, not even a ravaging wolf eating up my flesh!
I want spring, I want to turn like a mobile
In a new fresh air! I don't want to hibernate
Between walls, between halls! I want to bear
My share of the anguish of being succinctly here!
Not even moths in the spell of the flame
Can want it to be warmer so much as I do!
Not even the pilot slipping into the great green sea
In flames can want less to be turned to an icicle!
Though admiring the icicle's cunning, how shall I be satisfied
With artificial daisies and roses, and wax pears?
O breeze, my lovely, come in, that I mayn't be stultified!
Dear coolness of heaven, come swiftly and sit in my chairs!

To You

I love you as a sheriff searches for a walnut
That will solve a murder case unsolved for years
Because the murderer left it in the snow beside a window
Through which he saw her head, connecting with
Her shoulders by a neck, and laid a red
Roof in her heart. For this we live a thousand years;
For this we love, and we live because we love, we are not
Inside a bottle, thank goodness! I love you as a
Kid searches for a goat; I am crazier than shirttails
In the wind, when you're near, a wind that blows from
The big blue sea, so shiny so deep and so unlike us;
I think I am bicycling across an Africa of green and white fields
Always, to be near you, even in my heart
When I'm awake, which swims, and also I believe that you
Are trustworthy as the sidewalk which leads me to
The place where I again think of you, a new
Harmony of thoughts! I love you as the sunlight leads the prow
Of a ship which sails
From Hartford to Miami, and I love you
Best at dawn, when even before I am awake the sun
Receives me in the questions which you always pose.

Aus einer Kindheit

Is the basketball coach a homosexual lemon manufacturer? It is suspected
   by O'Ryan in his submarine.
When I was a child we always cried to be driven for a ride in that
   submarine. Daddy would say Yes!
Mommy would say No! The maid read *Anna Karenina* and told us
   secrets. Some suspected her of a liaison with O'Ryan. Nothing but
   squirrels
Seemed to be her interest, at the windows, except on holidays, like
   Easter and Thanksgiving, when
She would leave the basement and rave among the leaves, shouting, I am
   the Spirit of Softball! Come to me!
Daddy would always leave town. And a chorus of spiders
Would hang from my bedroom wall. Mommy had a hat made out of
   pasty hooks. She gave a party to limburger cheese.
We all were afraid that O'Ryan would come!
He came, he came! as the fall wind comes, waving and razing and
   swirling the leaves
With his bags, his moustache, his cigar, his golfball, his pencils, his April
   compasses, and over his whole
Body we children saw signs of life beneath the water! Oh!
Will he dance the hornpipe? we wondered, Will he smoke a cigar
   underneath eleven inches of ocean? Will he beat the pavement
Outside our door with his light feet, for being so firm? Is he a lemon
   Memnon?
O'Ryan O'Ryan O'Ryan! The maid came up from the basement, we
   were all astonished. And she said, "Is it Thanksgiving? Christmas? I
   felt
A force within me stir." And then she saw O'Ryan! The basketball
   coach followed her up from the cellar. He and O'Ryan fight!
No one is homosexual then! happily I swim through the bathtubs with
   my scarlet-haired sister
Z. ("O women I love you!" O'Ryan cried.) And we parked under
   water. Then, looking out the window,
We saw that snow had begun to fall, upon the green grass, and both
   shyly entered the new world of our bleached underwear. Rome!
   Rome!
Was our maid entertaining that limburger cheese, or my mother? has the

passageway fallen asleep? and can one's actions for six years be called "improper"?

I hope not. I hope the sea. I hope cigars will be smoked. I hope it from New York to California. From Tallahassee to St. Paul.

I hope the orange punching bag will be socked, and that you'll be satisfied, sweet friend. I hope international matrimony, lambent skies, and "Ship, ahoy!"

For we're due to be dawned on, I guess.

Spring

Let's take a walk
In the city
Till our shoes get wet
(It's been raining
All night) and when
We see the traffic
Lights and the moon
Let's take a smile
Off the ashcan, let's walk
Into town (I mean
A lemon peel)

Let's make music
(I hear the cats
Purply beautiful
Like hallways in summer
Made of snowing rubber
Valence piccalilli and diamonds)
Oh see the arch ruby
Of this late March sky
Are you less intelligent
Than the pirate of lemons
Let's take a walk

I know you tonight
As I have never known
A book of white stones
Or a bookcase of orange groans
Or symbolism
I think I'm in love
With those imaginary racetracks
Of red traced grey in
The sky and the gimcracks
Of all you know and love
Who once loathed firecrackers
And license plates and
Diamonds but now you love them all

And just for my sake
Let's take a walk
Into the river
(I can even do that
Tonight) where
If I kiss you please
Remember with your shoes off
You're so beautiful like
A lifted umbrella orange
And white we may never
Discover the blue over-
Coat maybe never never O blind
With this (love) let's walk
Into the first
Rivers of morning as you are seen
To be bathed in a light white light
Come on

In Love with You

O what a physical effect it has on me
To dive forever into the light blue sea
Of your acquaintance! Ah, but dearest friends,
Like forms, are finished, as life has ends! Still,
It is beautiful, when October
Is over, and February is over,
To sit in the starch of my shirt, and to dream of your sweet
Ways! As if the world were a taxi, you enter it, then
Reply (to no one), "Let's go five or six blocks."
Isn't the blue stream that runs past you a translation from the Russian?
Aren't my eyes bigger than love?
Isn't this history, and aren't we a couple of ruins?
Is Carthage Pompeii? is the pillow the bed? is the sun
What glues our heads together? O midnight! O midnight!
Is love what we are,
Or has happiness come to me in a private car
That's so very small I'm amazed to see it there?

2

We walk through the park in the sun, and you say, "There's a spider
Of shadow touching the bench, when morning's begun." I love you.
I love you fame I love you raining sun I love you cigarettes I love you
    love
I love you daggers I love smiles daggers and symbolism.

3

Inside the symposium of your sweetest look's
Sunflower awning by the nurse-faced chrysanthemums childhood
Again represents a summer spent sticking knives into porcelain
    raspberries, when China's
Still a country! Oh, King Edward abdicated years later, that's

Exactly when. If you were seventy thousand years old, and I were a pill,
I know I could cure your headache, like playing baseball in drinking
    water, as baskets
Of towels sweetly touch the bathroom floor! O benches of nothing
Appear and reappear—electricity! I'd love to be how
You are, as if
The world were new, and the selves were blue
Which we don
When it's dawn,
Until evening puts on
The gray hooded selves and the light brown selves of . . .
Water! your tear-colored nail polish
Kisses me! and the lumberyard seems new
As a calm
On the sea, where, like pigeons,
I feel so mutated, sad, so breezed, so revivified, and still so
    unabdicated—
Not like an edge of land coming over the sea!

Geography

In the blue hubbub of the same-through-wealth sky
Amba grew to health and fifteenth year among the jungle scrubbery.
The hate-bird sang on a lower wing of the birch-nut tree
And Amba heard him sing, and in his health he too
Began to sing, but then stopped. Along the lower Congo
There are such high plants of what there is there, when
At morning Amba heard their pink music as gentlemanly
As if he had been in civilization. When morning stank
Over the ridge of coconuts and bald fronds, with agility
Amba climbed the permanent nut trees, and will often sing
To the shining birds, and the pets in their stealth
Are each other among, also, whether it be blue (thhhh) feathers
Or green slumber. Africa in Amba's mind was those white mornings he
    sang
(thhhh) high trala to the nougat birds, and after
The trenches had all been dug for the day, Amba
Would dream at the edge of some stained and stinking pond
Of the afternight music, as blue pets came to him in his dreams;
From the orange coconuts he would extract some stained milk,
Underneath his feet roots, tangled and filthy green. At night
The moon (zzzzzz) shining down on Amba's sweet mocked sleep.

2

In Chicago Louis walked the morning's rounds with agility.
A boy of seventeen and already recognized as a fast milkman!
The whizz and burr of dead chimes oppressed the
Holocaustic unison of Frank's brain, a young outlaw
Destined to meet dishonor and truth in a same instant,
Crossing Louis' path gently in the street, the great secret unknown.

3

The fur rhubarb did not please Daisy. "Freddie," she called,
"Our fruit's gang mouldy." Daisy, white cheeks with a spot of red
In them, like apples grown in paper bags, smiled
Gently at the fresh new kitchen; and, then, depressed,
She began to cover the rhubarb with her hands.

4

In the crushy green ice and snow Baba ran up and around with
     exuberance!
Today, no doubt, Father and Uncle Dad would come, and together they
     three would chase the whale!
Baba stared down through the green crusty ice at the world of fish
And closed his eyes and began to imagine the sweet trip
Over the musky waters, when Daddy would spear the whale, and the
     wind
Blow "Crad, crad!" through Uncle Dad's fur, and the sweet end
Of the day where they would smile at one another over the smoking
     blubber
And Uncle Dad would tell tales of his adventures past the shadow bar
Chasing the white snow-eagle. Baba ran
Into the perfect igloo screaming with impatience, and Malmal,
His mother, kissed him and dressed him with loving care for the icy
     trip.

5

Ten Ko sprinted over the rice paddies. Slush, slosh, sloosh!
His brother, Wan Kai, would soon be returned from the village
Where he had gone . . . (Blue desire! . . .)

6

Roon startled her parents by appearing perfectly dressed
In a little white collar and gown.
Angebor lifted himself up so he might stare in the window at the pretty
  girl.
His little hands unclenched and dropped the coins he had saved for the
  oona.
He opened wide his eyes, then blinked at the pretty girl. He had never
  seen anything like that.
That evening, when it whitened in the sky, and a green
Clearness was there, Maggia and Angebor had no *oona*.
But Angebor talked with excitement of what he had seen, and Maggia
  drank *zee'th*.

7

The little prisoner wept and wailed, telling of his life in the sand
And the burning sun over the desert. And one night it was cool
And dark, and he stole away over the green sand to search for his
  parents.
And he went to their tent, and they kissed him and covered him with
  loving-kindness.
And the new morning sun shone like a pink rose in the heavens,
And the family prayed, the desert wind scorching their cool skin.

8

Amba arose. Thhhhhhh! went the birds, and clink clank cleck went
The leaves under the monkeys' feet, and Amba went to search for water
Speaking quietly with his fresh voice as he went toward Gorilla Lake
To all the beasts. Wan Kai lifted his body from the rice mat
When his brother Ten Ko came running in. "They have agreed in the
  village,"
He said. Win Tei brought them tea. Outside the rain

17

Fell. Plop, plop. Daisy felt something stir inside her.

She went to the window and looked out at the snow. Louis came up the stairs

With the milk. "Roon has bronchitis," said the American doctor,

"She will have to stay inside for ten days during this rain." Amba

Sneaked away, and wanted to go there again, but Maggia said he could not go again in this rain

And would be sure to lose the money for the *oona*. Baba stared

At the green and black sea. Uncle Dad stood up in the boat, while Baba

Watched Father plunge his harpoon three times in the whale. Daisy turned

Dreamily around, her hand on her cheek. Frank's boot

Kicked in the door. Amba wept; Ahna the deer was dead; she lay amid her puzzled young.

The sweet forms of the apple blossoms bent down to Wehtukai.

The boat split. Sun streamed into the apartment. Amba, Amba!

The lake was covered with gloom. Enna plunged into it screaming.

The Circus

1

We will have to go away, said the girls in the circus
And never come back any more. There is not enough of an audience
In this little town. Waiting against the black, blue sky
The big circus chariots took them into their entrances.
The light rang out over the hill where the circus wagons dimmed away.
Underneath their dresses the circus girls were sweating,
But then, an orange tight sticking to her, one spoke with
Blue eyes, she was young and pretty, blonde
With bright eyes, and she spoke with her mouth open when she sneezed
Lightly against the backs of the other girls waiting in line
To clock the rope, or come spinning down with her teeth on the line,
And she said that the circus might leave—and red posters
Stuck to the outside of the wagon, it was beginning to
Rain—she said might leave but not her heart would ever leave
Not that town but just any one where they had been, risking their lives,
And that each place they were should be celebrated by blue rosemary
In a patch, in the town. But they laughed and said Sentimental
Blonde, and she laughed, and they all, circus girls, clinging
To each other as the circus wagons rushed through the night.

2

In the next wagon, the one forward of theirs, the next wagon
Was the elephants' wagon. A grey trunk dragged on the floor . . .

3

Orville the Midget tramped up and down. Paul the Separated Man
Leaped forward. It rained and rained. Some people in the cities
Where they passed through were sitting behind thick glass
Windows, talking about their brats and drinking chocolate syrup.

4

Minnie the Rabbit fingered her machine gun.
The bright day was golden.
She aimed the immense pine needle at the foxes
Thinking Now they will never hurt my tribe any more.

5

The circus wagons stopped during the night
For eighteen minutes in a little town called Rosebud, Nebraska.
It was after dinner it was after bedtime it was after nausea it was
After lunchroom. The girls came out and touched each other and had
  fun
And just had time to get a breath of the fresh air of the night in
Before the ungodly procession began once more down the purple
  highway.

6

With what pomp and ceremony the circus arrived orange and red in the
  dawn!
It was exhausted, cars and wagons, and it lay down and leaped
Forward a little bit, like a fox. Minnie the Rabbit shot a little woolen
  bullet at it,
And just then the elephant man came to his doorway in the sunlight and
  stood still.

7

The snoring circus master wakes up, he takes it on himself to arrange the
  circus.
Soon the big tent floats high. Birds sing on the tent.
The parade girls and the living statue girls and the trapeze girls

Cover their sweet young bodies with phosphorescent paint.
Some of the circus girls are older women, but each is beautiful.
They stand, waiting for their cues, at the doorway of the tent.
The sky-blue lion tamer comes in, and the red giraffe manager.
They are very brave and wistful, and they look at the girls.
Some of the circus girls feel a hot sweet longing in their bodies.
But now is it time for the elephants!
Slowly the giant beasts march in. Some of their legs are clothed in blue
    papier-mâché ruffles.
One has a red eye. The elephant man is at the peak of happiness.
He speaks, giddily, to every one of the circus people he passes,
He does not know what he is saying, he does not care—
His elephants are on display! They walk into the sandy ring . . .

8

Suddenly a great scream breaks out in the circus tent!
It is Aileen the trapeze artist, she has fallen into the dust and dirt
From so high! She must be dead! The stretcher bearers rush out,
They see her lovely human form clothed in red and white and orange
    wiry net,
And they see that she does not breathe any more.
The circus doctor leaves his tent, he runs out to care for Aileen.
He traverses the circus grounds and the dusty floor of the circus entrance,
    and he comes
Where she is, now she has begun to move again, she is not dead,
But the doctor tells her he does not know if she will ever be able to
    perform on the trapeze again,
And he sees the beautiful orange and red and white form shaken with
    sobs,
And he puts his hand on her forehead and tells her she must lie still.

9

The circus girls form a cortege, they stand in file in the yellow and
    white sunlight.

"What is death in the circus? That depends on if it is spring.
Then, if elephants are there, *mon père,* we are not completely lost.
Oh the sweet strong odor of beasts which laughs at decay!
Decay! decay! We are like the elements in a kaleidoscope,
But such passions we feel! bigger than beaches and
Rustier than harpoons." After his speech the circus practitioner sat down.

10

Minnie the Rabbit felt the blood leaving her little body
As she lay in the snow, orange and red and white,
A beautiful design. The dog laughs, his tongue hangs out, he looks at
    the sky.
It is white. The master comes. He laughs. He picks up Minnie the
    Rabbit
And ties her to a pine tree bough, and leaves.

11

Soon through the forest came the impassioned bumble bee.
He saw the white form on the bough. "Like rosebuds when you are
    thirteen," said Elmer.
Iris noticed that he didn't have any cap on.
"You must be polite when mother comes," she said.
The sky began to get grey, then the snow came.
The two tots pressed together. Elmer opened his mouth and let the snow
    fall in it. Iris felt warm and happy.

12

Bang! went the flyswatter. Mr. Watkins, the circus manager, looked
    around the room.
"Damn it, damn these flies!" he said. Mr. Loftus, the circus clerk, stared
    at the fly interior he had just exposed.

22

The circus doctor stood beside the lake. In his hand he had a black
briefcase.
A wind ruffled the surface of the lake and slightly rocked the boats.

Red and green fish swam beneath the surface of the water.
The doctor went into the lunchroom and sat down. No, he said, he
didn't care for anything to eat.
The soft wind of summer blew in the light green trees.

Collected Poems

BUFFALO DAYS

I was asleep when you waked up the buffalo.

THE ORANGE WIVES

A mountain of funny foam went past.

GREAT HUMAN VOICES

The starlit voices drip.

COLORFUL HOUR

A few green pencils in a born pocket.

EXPRESSION

New little tray.

SLEEP

The bantam hen frayed its passage through the soft clouds.

A MINERAL WICK

Town soda.

SOMEWHERE

Between islands and envy.

CECELIA

Look, a cat.

THE SILVER WORLD

Expands.

JEWELRY SEVENTHS

Minor wonders.

AN ESKIMO COCA COLA

Three-fifths.

THE EXCEPTION PROVES THE RULE

Eight-fifths.
Nine-fifths.
Three-fifths.
Six-fifths.

THE WATER HOSE IS ON FIRE

Grapeline.

THE LINGERING MATADORS

Eskimo City.

EGYPT

Passiveness.

IS THERE A HOUSE INSIDE THAT FUEL ENGINE?

Extra aging will bring your craft over against the rosy skies.

WHY WEREN'T THEY MORE CAREFUL?

Actions.

PEANUT BUTTER CANDY

Ichthious.

THE BRINDLE COWS

Dairy farm, dairy farm,
H-O-T
H-E-A-D.

IN THE MERRY FOAM

Ask them for the blue patience of lovers.

MY MIXUP

The cherries after a shower.

MILKWEED EMBLEMS

The chambered nautilus is weak.

SUPPOSE

Red and white riding hoods.

THE GREEN MEDDLER

Aged in the fire.

A HOUSE IN MISSISSIPPI

Who stole all my new sander supplies?

WICKED OBJECTS

Aeroliths.

FRESH LIMES

A couple's bedroom slippers.

THE WINDOW

The chimney.

PAINTED FOR A ROSE

The exacting pilgrims were delighted with yellow fatigue.

NOONS

Bubbles.

ROOMS

Simplex bumblebees.

IN THE RANCHHOUSE AT DAWN

O corpuscle!
O wax town!

THE OUTSIDES OF THINGS

The sky fold, and then the bus started up.

THE BLACK LION

Never stop revealing yourself.

IN THE COAL MUD

At breakfast we could sob.

THE HAND-PAINTED EARS OF DEATH

Oh look inside me.

ALABAMA

Alabama!

The Artist

Ah, well, I abandon you, cherrywood smokestack,
Near the entrance to this old green park! . . .

     *   *   *

Cherrywood avalanche, my statue of you
Is still standing in Toledo, Ohio.
O places, summer, boredom, the static of an acrobatic blue!

And I made an amazing zinc airliner
It is standing to this day in the Minneapolis zoo . . .

Old times are not so long ago, plaster of Paris haircut!

     *   *   *

I often think *Play* was my best work.
It is an open field with a few boards in it.

Children are allowed to come and play in *Play*
By permission of the Cleveland Museum.
I look up at the white clouds, I wonder what I shall do, and smile.

Perhaps somebody will grow up having been influenced by *Play*,
I think—but what good will that do?
Meanwhile I am interested in steel cigarettes . . .

     *   *   *

The orders are coming in thick and fast for steel cigarettes, steel cigars.
The Indianapolis Museum has requested six dozen packages.
I wonder if I'd still have the courage to do a thing like *Play?*

I think I may go to Cleveland . . .

     *   *   *

Well, here I am! Pardon me, can you tell me how to get to the
 Cleveland Museum's monumental area, *Play?*
"Mister, that was torn down a long time ago. You ought to go and see
 the new thing they have now—*Gun.*"
What? *Play* torn down?
"Yes, Mister, and I loved to climb in it too, when I was a kid!" And he
 shakes his head
Sadly . . . But I am thrilled beyond expectation!
He liked my work!
And I guess there must be others like that man in Cleveland too . . .

So you see, *Play* has really had its effect!
Now I am on the outskirts of town
And . . . here it is! But it has changed! There are some blue merds lying
 in the field
And it's not marked *Play* anymore—and here's a calf!
I'm so happy, I can't tell why!
Was this how I originally imagined *Play,* but lacked the courage?

It would be hard now, though, to sell it to another museum.
I wonder if the man I met's children will come and play in it?
How does one's audience survive?

*   *   *

Pittsburgh, May 16th. I have abandoned the steel cigarettes. I am
 working on *Bee.*
Bee will be a sixty-yards-long covering for the elevator shaft opening in
 the foundry sub-basement
Near my home. So far it's white sailcloth with streams of golden paint
 evenly spaced out
With a small blue pond at one end, and around it orange and green
 flowers. My experience in Cleveland affected me so
That my throat aches whenever I am not working at full speed. I have
 never been so happy and inspired and
Play seems to me now like a juvenile experience!

29

*   *   *

June 8th. *Bee* is still not finished. I have introduced a huge number of
   red balloons into it. How will it work?
Yesterday X. said, "Are you still working on *Bee?* What's happened to
   your interest in steel cigarettes?"
Y. said, "He hasn't been doing any work at all on them since he went to
   Cleveland." A shrewd guess! But how much can they possibly know?

*   *   *

November 19th. Disaster! *Bee* was almost completed, and now the
   immense central piece of sailcloth has torn. Impossible to repair it!

December 4th. I've gone back to work on *Bee!* I suddenly thought (after
   weeks of despair!), "I can place the balloons over the tear in the
   canvas!" So that is what I am doing. All promises to be well!

December 6th. The foreman of the foundry wants to look at my work.
   It seems that he too is an "artist"—does sketches and watercolors and
   such . . . What will he think of *Bee?*

*   *   *

Cherrywood! I had left you far from my home
And the foreman came to look at *Bee*
And the zinc airliner flew into *Play!*

The pink balloons aren't heavy, but the yellow ones break.
The foreman says, "It's the greatest thing I ever saw!"
Cleveland heard too and wants me to come back and reinaugurate *Play*

I dream of going to Cleveland but never will
Bee has obsessed my mind.

*   *   *

March 14th. A cold spring day. It is snowing. *Bee* is completed.

      *   *   *

O *Bee* I think you are my best work
In the blue snow-filled air
I feel my heart break
I lie down in the snow
They come from the foundry and take *Bee* away
Oh what can I create now, Earth,

Green Earth on which everything blossoms anew?
"A bathroom floor cardboard trolley line
The shape and size of a lemon seed with on the inside
A passenger the size of a pomegranate seed
Who is an invalid and has to lean on the cardboard side
Of the lemon-seed-sized trolley line so that he won't fall off the train."

      *   *   *

I just found these notes written many years ago.
How seriously I always take myself! Let it be a lesson to me.
To bring things up to date: I have just finished *Campaign,* which is a
    tremendous piece of charcoal.
Its shape is difficult to describe; but it is extremely large and would
    reach to the sixth floor of the Empire State Building. I have been
    very successful in the past fourteen or fifteen years.

      *   *   *

Summer Night, shall I never succeed in finishing you? Oh you are the
    absolute end of all my creation! The ethereal beauty of that
    practically infinite number of white stone slabs stretching into the blue
    secrecy of ink! O stabs in my heart!

. . . . Why not a work *Stabs in My Heart?* But *Summer Night?*

31

January. . . . A troubled sleep. Can I make two things at once? What
way is there to be sure that the impulse to work on *Stabs in My Heart*
is serious? It seems occasioned only by my problem about finishing
Summer Night . . . ?

*   *   *

The *Magician of Cincinnati* is now ready for human use. They are
twenty-five tremendous stone staircases, each over six hundred feet high,
which will be placed in the Ohio River between Cincinnati and
Louisville, Kentucky. All the boats coming down the Ohio River will
presumably be smashed up against the immense statues, which are the
most recent work of the creator of *Flowers, Bee, Play, Again* and *Human
Use.* Five thousand citizens are thronged on the banks of the Ohio
waiting to see the installation of the work, and the crowd is expected to
be more than fifteen times its present number before morning. There will
be a game of water baseball in the early afternoon, before the beginning
of the ceremonies, between the Cincinnati Redlegs and the Pittsburgh
Pirates. The *Magician of Cincinnati,* incidentally, is said to be absolutely
impregnable to destruction of any kind, and will therefore presumably
always be a feature of this part of the Ohio. . . .

*   *   *

May 16th. With what an intense joy I watched the installation of the
Magician of Cincinnati today, in the Ohio River, where it belongs, and
which is so much a part of my original scheme. . . .

May 17th. I feel suddenly freed from life—not so much as if my work
were going to change, but as though I had at last seen what I had so
long been prevented (perhaps I prevented myself!) from seeing: that
there is too much for me to do. Somehow this enables me to relax, to
breathe easily. . . .

*   *   *

There's the *Magician of Cincinnati*

In the distance
Here I am in the green trees of Pennsylvania

How strange I felt when they had installed
The *Magician!* . . . Now a bluebird trills, I am busy making my polished
    stones
For *Dresser.*

The stream the stone the birds the reddish-pink Pennsylvania hills
All go to make up *Dresser*
Why am I camping out?
I am waiting for the thousands of tons of embalming fluid
That have to come and with which I can make these hills.

        *   *   *

GREATEST ARTISTIC EVENT HINTED BY GOVERNOR
Reading, June 4. Greatest artistic event was hinted today by governor.
    Animals converge on meadow where artist working.

CONVERGE ON MEADOW WHERE WORKING

ARTIST HINTED, SAME MAN

. . . the *Magician of Cincinnati*

THREE YEARS

October 14th. I want these hills to be striated! How naive the *Magician
    of Cincinnati* was! Though it makes me happy to think of it. . . .
    Here, I am plunged into such real earth! Striate, hills! What is this
    deer's head of green stone? I can't fabricate anything less than what I
    think should girdle the earth. . . .

PHOTOGRAPH

PHOTOGRAPH

PHOTOGRAPH

Artist who created the *Magician of Cincinnati;* Now at work in Pennsylvania; The Project—*Dresser*—So Far.

    *   *   *

Ah! . . .

    *   *   *

TONS

SILICON, GRASS AND DEER-HEAD RANGE
Philadelphia. Your voice as well as mine will be appreciated to express the appreciation of *Dresser,* which makes of Pennsylvania the silicon, grass and stone-deer-head center of the world. . . . Artist says he may change his mind about the central bridges. Fountains to give forth real tar-water. Mountain lake in center. Real chalk cliffs. Also cliffs of clay. Deep declivities nearby. "Wanted forest atmosphere, yet to be open." Gas . . .

    *   *   *

PHOTOGRAPH

SKETCH

DEDICATION CEREMONY

GOES SWIMMING IN OWN STREAM

SHAKING HANDS WITH GOVERNOR

COLOR PICTURE

THE HEAD OF THE ARTIST

THE ARTIST'S HAND

STACK OF ACTUAL BILLS NEEDED TO PAY FOR PROJECT

Story of *Dresser*

PENNSYLVANIA'S PRIDE: *DRESSER*

Creator of *Dresser*

*　　*　　*

STILL SMILING AT FORGE
Beverly, South Dakota, April 18. Still smiling at forge, artist of *Dresser* says, "No, of course I haven't forgotten *Dresser*. Though how quickly the years have gone by since I have been doing *Too!*" We glanced up at the sky and saw a large white bird, somewhat similar to an immense seagull, which was as if fixed above our heads. Its eyes were blue sapphires, and its wings were formed by an ingenious arrangement of whitened daffodil-blossom parts. Its body seemed mainly charcoal, on the whole, with a good deal of sand mixed in. As we watched it, the creature actually seemed to move. . . .

August 4th . . . Three four five, and it's finished! I can see it in
　Beverly . . .

*　　*　　*

BEVERLY HONORS ARTIST. CALLED "FOUNDING FATHER"

Beverly, South Dakota, August 14 . . .

MISSISSIPPI CLAIMS BIRTHPLACE

HONORS BIRTHPLACE

BIRTHPLACE HONORS HELD

35

*   *   *

INDIANS AND SAVANTS MEET TO PRAISE *WEST WIND*

PAT HONORED

PAT AND *WEST WIND* HONORED

*   *   *

June 3rd. It doesn't seem possible—the Pacific Ocean! I have ordered sixteen
million tons of blue paint. Waiting anxiously for it to arrive.
How would grass be as a substitute? cement?

*   *   *

Fresh Air

I

At the Poem Society a black-haired man stands up to say
"You make me sick with all your talk about restraint and mature talent!
Haven't you ever looked out the window at a painting by Matisse,
Or did you always stay in hotels where there were too many spiders
    crawling on your visages?
Did you ever glance inside a bottle of sparkling pop,
Or see a citizen split in two by the lightning?
I am afraid you have never smiled at the hibernation
Of bear cubs except that you saw in it some deep relation
To human suffering and wishes, oh what a bunch of crackpots!"
The black-haired man sits down, and the others shoot arrows at him.
A blond man stands up and says,
"He is right! Why should we be organized to defend the kingdom
Of dullness? There are so many slimy people connected with poetry,
Too, and people who know nothing about it!
I am not recommending that poets like each other and organize to fight
    them,
But simply that lightning should strike them."
Then the assembled mediocrities shot arrows at the blond-haired man.
The chairman stood up on the platform, oh he was physically ugly!
He was small-limbed and -boned and thought he was quite seductive,
But he was bald with certain hideous black hairs,
And his voice had the sound of water leaving a vaseline bathtub,
And he said, "The subject for this evening's discussion is poetry
On the subject of love between swans." And everyone threw candy
    hearts
At the disgusting man, and they stuck to his bib and tucker,
And he danced up and down on the platform in terrific glee
And recited the poetry of his little friends—but the blond man stuck his
    head
Out of a cloud and recited poems about the east and thunder,
And the black-haired man moved through the stratosphere chanting
Poems of the relationships between terrific prehistoric charcoal whales,
And the slimy man with candy hearts sticking all over him
Wilted away like a cigarette paper on which the bumblebees have
    urinated,

And all the professors left the room to go back to their duty,
And all that were left in the room were five or six poets
And together they sang the new poem of the twentieth century
Which, though influenced by Mallarmé, Shelley, Byron, and Whitman,
Plus a million other poets, is still entirely original
And is so exciting that it cannot be here repeated.
You must go to the Poem Society and wait for it to happen.
Once you have heard this poem you will not love any other,
Once you have dreamed this dream you will be inconsolable,
Once you have loved this dream you will be as one dead,
Once you have visited the passages of this time's great art!

2

"Oh to be seventeen years old
Once again," sang the red-haired man, "and not know that poetry
Is ruled with the sceptre of the dumb, the deaf, and the creepy!"
And the shouting persons battered his immortal body with stones
And threw his primitive comedy into the sea
From which it sang forth poems irrevocably blue.

Who are the great poets of our time, and what are their names?
Yeats of the baleful influence, Auden of the baleful influence, Eliot of
    the baleful influence
(Is Eliot a great poet? no one knows), Hardy, Stevens, Williams (is
    Hardy of our time?),
Hopkins (is Hopkins of our time?), Rilke (is Rilke of our time?), Lorca
    (is Lorca of our time?), who is still of our time?
Mallarmé, Valéry, Apollinaire, Éluard, Reverdy, French poets are still of
    our time,
Pasternak and Mayakovsky, is Jouve of our time?

Where are young poets in America, they are trembling in publishing
    houses and universities,
Above all they are trembling in universities, they are bathing the library
    steps with their spit,

They are gargling out innocuous (to whom?) poems about maple trees
 and their children,
Sometimes they brave a subject like the Villa d'Este or a lighthouse in
 Rhode Island,
Oh what worms they are! They wish to perfect their form.

Yet could not these young men, put in another profession,
Succeed admirably, say at sailing a ship? I do not doubt it, Sir, and I
 wish we could try them.
(A plane flies over the ship holding a bomb but perhaps it will not drop
 the bomb,
The young poets from the universities are staring anxiously at the skies,
Oh they are remembering their days on the campus when they looked
 up to watch birds excrete,
They are remembering the days they spent making their elegant poems.)

Is there no voice to cry out from the wind and say what it is like to be
 the wind,
To be roughed up by the trees and to bring music from the scattered
 houses
And the stones, and to be in such intimate relationship with the sea
That you cannot understand it? Is there no one who feels like a pair of
 pants?

3

Summer in the trees! "It is time to strangle several bad poets."
The yellow hobbyhorse rocks to and fro, and from the chimney
Drops the Strangler! The white and pink roses are slightly agitated by
 the struggle,
But afterwards beside the dead "poet" they cuddle up comfortingly
 against their vase. They are safer now, no one will compare them to
 the sea.

Here on the railroad train, one more time, is the Strangler.
He is going to get that one there, who is on his way to a poetry
 reading.

Agh! Biff! A body falls to the moving floor.

In the football stadium I also see him,
He leaps through the frosty air at the maker of comparisons
Between football and life and silently, silently strangles him!

Here is the Strangler dressed in a cowboy suit
Leaping from his horse to annihilate the students of myth!

The Strangler's ear is alert for the names of Orpheus,
Cuchulain, Gawain, and Odysseus,
And for poems addressed to Jane Austen, F. Scott Fitzgerald,
To Ezra Pound, and to personages no longer living
Even in anyone's thoughts—O Strangler the Strangler!

He lies on his back in the waves of the Pacific Ocean.

4

Supposing that one walks out into the air
On a fresh spring day and has the misfortune
To encounter an article on modern poetry
In *New World Writing,* or has the misfortune
To see some examples of some of the poetry
Written by the men with their eyes on the myth
And the Missus and the midterms, in the *Hudson Review,*
Or, if one is abroad, in *Botteghe Oscure,*
Or indeed in *Encounter,* what is one to do
With the rest of one's day that lies blasted to ruins
All bluely about one, what is one to do?
Oh surely one cannot complain to the President,
Nor even to the deans of Columbia College,
Nor to T. S. Eliot, nor to Ezra Pound,
And supposing one writes to the Princess Caetani,
"Your poets are awful!" what good would it do?
And supposing one goes to the *Hudson Review*

With a package of matches and sets fire to the building?
One ends up in prison with trial subscriptions
To the *Partisan, Sewanee,* and *Kenyon Review*!

5

Sun out! perhaps there is a reason for the lack of poetry
In these ill-contented souls, perhaps they need air!

Blue air, fresh air, come in, I welcome you, you are an art student,
Take off your cap and gown and sit down on the chair.
Together we shall paint the poets—but no, air! perhaps you should go
  to them, quickly,
Give them a little inspiration, they need it, perhaps they are out of
  breath,
Give them a little inhuman company before they freeze the English
  language to death!
(And rust their typewriters a little, be sea air! be noxious! kill them, if
  you must, but stop their poetry!
I remember I saw you dancing on the surf on the Côte d'Azur,
And I stopped, taking my hat off, but you did not remember me,
Then afterwards you came to my room bearing a handful of orange
  flowers
And we were together all through the summer night!)

That we might go away together, it is so beautiful on the sea, there are
  a few white clouds in the sky!

But no, air! you must go . . . Ah, stay!

But she has departed and . . . Ugh! what poisonous fumes and clouds!
  what a suffocating atmosphere!
Cough! whose are these hideous faces I see, what is this rigor
Infecting the mind? where are the green Azores,
Fond memories of childhood, and the pleasant orange trolleys,
A girl's face, red-white, and her breasts and calves, blue eyes, brown
  eyes, green eyes, fahrenheit

Temperatures, dandelions, and trains, O blue?!

Wind, wind, what is happening? Wind! I can't see any bird but the gull,
and I feel it should symbolize . . .

Oh, pardon me, there's a swan, one two three swans, a great white swan,
hahaha how pretty they are! Smack!

Oh! stop! help! yes, I see—disrespect for my superiors—forgive me,
dear Zeus, nice Zeus, parabolic bird, O feathered excellence! white!

There is Achilles too, and there's Ulysses, I've always wanted to see
them,

And there is Helen of Troy, I suppose she is Zeus too, she's so terribly
pretty—hello, Zeus, my you are beautiful, Bang!

One more mistake and I get thrown out of the Modern Poetry
Association, help! Why aren't there any adjectives around?

Oh there are, there's practically nothing else—look, here's *grey, utter,
agonized, total, phenomenal, gracile, invidious, sundered,* and *fused,*

Elegant, absolute, pyramidal, and . . . Scream! but what can I describe
with these words? States!

States symbolized and divided by two, complex states, magic states, states
of consciousness governed by an aroused sincerity, cockadoodle doo!

Another bird! is it morning? Help! where am I? am I in the barnyard?
oink oink, scratch, moo! Splash!

My first lesson. "Look around you. What do you think and feel?" *Uhhh*
. . . "Quickly!" *This Connecticut landscape would have pleased Vermeer.*
Wham! A-Plus. "Congratulations!" I am promoted.

OOOhhhhh I wish I were dead, what a headache! My second lesson:
"Rewrite your first lesson line six hundred times. Try to make it into
a magnetic field." I can do it too. But my poor line! What a
nightmare! Here comes a tremendous horse.

Trojan, I presume. No, it's my third lesson. "Look, look! Watch him,
see what he's doing? That's what we want you to do. Of course it
won't be the same as his at first, but . . ." I demur. Is there no other
way to fertilize minds?

Bang! I give in . . . Already I see my name in two or three anthologies,
a serving girl comes into the barn bringing me the anthologies,

She is very pretty and I smile at her a little sadly, perhaps it is my last
smile! Perhaps she will hit me! But no, she smiles in return, and she
takes my hand.

My hand, my hand! what is this strange thing I feel in my hand, on my
   arm, on my chest, my face—can it be . . . ? it is! AIR!
Air, air, you've come back! Did you have any success? "What do you
   think?" I don't know, air. You are so strong, air.
And she breaks my chains of straw, and we walk down the road, behind
   us the hideous fumes!
Soon we reach the seaside, she is a young art student who places her
   head on my shoulder,
I kiss her warm red lips, and here is the Strangler, reading the *Kenyon
   Review!* Good luck to you, Strangler!
Goodbye, Helen! goodbye, fumes! goodbye, abstracted dried-up boys!
   goodbye, dead trees! goodbye, skunks!
Goodbye, manure! goodbye, critical manicure! goodbye, you big fat men
   standing on the east coast as well as the west giving poems the test!
   farewell, Valéry's stern dictum!
Until tomorrow, then, scum floating on the surface of poetry! goodbye
   for a moment, refuse that happens to land in poetry's boundaries!
   adieu, stale eggs teaching imbeciles poetry to bolster up your egos!
   adios, boring anomalies of these same stale eggs!
Ah, but the scum is deep! Come, let me help you! and soon we pass
   into the clear blue water. Oh GOODBYE, castrati of poetry!
   farewell, stale pale skunky pentameters (the only honest English meter,
   gloop gloop!)! until tomorrow, horrors! oh, farewell!

Hello, sea! good morning, sea! hello, clarity and excitement, you great
   expanse of green—

O green, beneath which all of them shall drown!

Thanksgiving

What's sweeter than at the end of a summer's day
To suddenly drift away
From the green match-wrappers in an opened pocketbook
And be part of the boards in a tavern?

A tavern made of new wood.
There's an orange-red sun in the sky
And a redskin is hunting for you underneath ladders of timber.
I will buy this tavern. Will you buy this tavern? I do.

In the Indian camp there's awful dismay.
Do they know us as we know they
Know us or will know us, I mean a—
I mean a hostile force, the month of May.

How whitely the springtime is blossoming,
Ugh! all around us!
It is the brilliant Indian time of year
When the sweetest Indians mate with the sweetest others.

But I fear the white men, I fear
The rent apple blossoms and discarded feathers
And the scalp lying secretly on the ground
Like an unoffending nose!

But we've destroyed all that. With shocking guns.
Peter Stuyvesant, Johnny Appleseed,
We've destroyed all that. Come,
Do you believe right was on either side?

How would you like to be living in an Indian America,
With feathers dressing every head? We'd eat buffalo hump
For Thanksgiving dinner. Everyone is in a tribe.
A girl from the Bep Tribe can't marry a brave from the Bap Tribe. Is
    that democracy?

And then those dreary evenings around the campfires

Listening to the Chief! If there were a New York
It would be a city of tents, and what do you suppose
Our art and poetry would be like? For the community! the tribe!
No beautiful modern abstract pictures, no mad incomprehensible
Free lovable poems! And our moral sense! tribal.
If you would like to be living in an Indian America
Why not subscribe to this newspaper, *Indian America?*

In Wisconsin, Ben, I stand, I walk up and down and try to decide.

Is this country getting any better or has it gotten?
If the Indian New York is bad, what about our white New York?
Dirty, unwholesome, the filthy appendage to a vast ammunition works, I
    hate it!
Disgusting rectangular garbage dump sending its fumes up to suffocate
    the sky—
Foo, what fumes! and the scaly white complexion of her citizens.
There's hell in every firm handshake, and stifled rage in every look.
If you do find somewhere to lie down, it's a dirty inspected corner,
And there are newspapers and forums and the stinking breath of
    Broadway
To investigate what it feels like to be a source of stench
And nothing else. And if one does go away,
It is always here, waiting, for one to come back. And one does come
    back,
As one comes back to the bathroom, and to a time of suffering.

Where else would I find such ardent and graceful spirits
Inspired and wasted and using and used by this horrible city,
New York, New York? Can the Pilgrims' Thanksgiving dinner really
    compare to it?
And the Puritans? And the single-minded ankle-divided Indians?
No, nothing can compare to it! So it's here we speak from the heart,
And it's rotting so fast that what we say
Fades like the last of a summer's day,
Rot which makes us prolific as the sun on white unfastened clouds.

Permanently

One day the Nouns were clustered in the street.
An Adjective walked by, with her dark beauty.
The Nouns were struck, moved, changed.
The next day a Verb drove up, and created the Sentence.

Each Sentence says one thing—for example, "Although it was a dark
   rainy day when the Adjective walked by, I shall remember the pure
   and sweet expression on her face until the day I perish from the
   green, effective earth."
Or, "Will you please close the window, Andrew?"
Or, for example, "Thank you, the pink pot of flowers on the window
   sill has changed color recently to a light yellow, due to the heat from
   the boiler factory which exists nearby."

In the springtime the Sentences and the Nouns lay silently on the grass.
A lonely Conjunction here and there would call, "And! But!"
But the Adjective did not emerge.

As the adjective is lost in the sentence,
So I am lost in your eyes, ears, nose, and throat—
You have enchanted me with a single kiss
Which can never be undone
Until the destruction of language.

Down at the Docks

Down at the docks
Where everything is sweet and inclines
At night
To the sound of canoes
I planted a maple tree
And every night
Beneath it I studied the cosmos
Down at the docks.

Sweet ladies, listen to me.
The dock is made of wood
The maple tree's not made of wood
It is wood
Wood comes from it
As music comes from me
And from this mandolin I've made
Out of the maple tree.

Jealous gentlemen, study how
Wood comes from the maple
Then devise your love
So that it seems
To come from where
All is it yet something more
White spring flowers and leafy bough
Jealous gentlemen.

Arrogant little waves
Knocking at the dock
It's for you I've made this chanson
For you and that big dark blue.

You Were Wearing

You were wearing your Edgar Allan Poe printed cotton blouse.
In each divided up square of the blouse was a picture of Edgar Allan
    Poe.
Your hair was blonde and you were cute. You asked me, "Do most boys
    think that most girls are bad?"
I smelled the mould of your seaside resort hotel bedroom on your hair
    held in place by a John Greenleaf Whittier clip.
"No," I said, "it's girls who think that boys are bad." Then we read
    Snowbound together
And ran around in an attic, so that a little of the blue enamel was
    scraped off my George Washington, Father of His Country, shoes.

Mother was walking in the living room, her Strauss Waltzes comb in
    her hair.
We waited for a time and then joined her, only to be served tea in cups
    painted with pictures of Herman Melville
As well as with illustrations from his book *Moby Dick* and from his
    novella, *Benito Cereno.*
Father came in wearing his Dick Tracy necktie: "How about a drink,
    everyone?"
I said, "Let's go outside a while." Then we went onto the porch and sat
    on the Abraham Lincoln swing.
You sat on the eyes, mouth, and beard part, and I sat on the knees.
In the yard across the street we saw a snowman holding a garbage can
    lid smashed into a likeness of the mad English king, George the
    Third.

Locks

These locks on doors have brought me happiness:
The lock on the door of the sewing machine in the living room
Of a tiny hut in which I was living with a mad seamstress;
The lock on the filling station one night when I was drunk
And had the idea of enjoying a nip of petroleum;
The lock on the family of seals, which, when released, would have
    bitten;
The lock on the life raft when I was taking a bath instead of drowning;
The lock inside the nose of the contemporary composer who was
    playing the piano and would have ruined his concert by sneezing,
    while I was turning pages;
The lock on the second hump of a camel while I was not running out
    of water in the desert;
The lock on the fish hatchery the night we came up from the beach
And were trying to find a place to spend the night—it was full of
    contagious fish;
The lock on my new necktie when I was walking through a stiff wind
On my way to an appointment at which I had to look neat and simple;
The lock on the foghorn the night of the lipstick parade—
If the foghorn had sounded, everyone would have run inside before the
    most beautiful contestant appeared;
The lock in my hat when I saw her and which kept me from tipping it,
Which she would not have liked, because she believed that naturalness
    was the most friendly;
The lock on the city in which we would not have met anyone we
    knew;
The lock on the airplane which was flying without a pilot
Above Miami Beach on the night when I unlocked my bones
To the wind, and let the gales of sweetness blow through me till I
    shuddered and shook
Like a key in a freezing hand, and ran up into the Miami night air like
    a stone;
The lock on the hayfield, which kept me from getting out of bed
To meet the hayfield committee there; the lock on the barn, that kept
    the piled-up hay away from me;
The lock on the mailboat that kept it from becoming a raincoat
On the night of the thunderstorm; the lock on the sailboat

That keeps it from taking me away from you when I am asleep with
   you,
And, when I am not, the lock on my sleep, that keeps me from waking
   and finding you are not there.

Variations on a Theme by
William Carlos Williams

I

I chopped down the house that you had been saving to live in next
   summer.
I am sorry, but it was morning, and I had nothing to do
and its wooden beams were so inviting.

2

We laughed at the hollyhocks together
and then I sprayed them with lye.
Forgive me. I simply do not know what I am doing.

3

I gave away the money that you had been saving to live on for the next
   ten years.
The man who asked for it was shabby
and the firm March wind on the porch was so juicy and cold.

4

Last evening we went dancing and I broke your leg.
Forgive me. I was clumsy, and
I wanted you here in the wards, where I am the doctor!

Thank You

Oh thank you for giving me the chance
Of being ship's doctor! I am sorry that I shall have to refuse—
But, you see, the most I know of medicine is orange flowers
Tilted in the evening light against a cashmere red
Inside which breasts invent the laws of light
And of night, where cashmere moors itself across the sea.
And thank you for giving me these quintuplets
To rear and make happy . . . My mind was on something else.

Thank you for giving me this battleship to wash,
But I have a rash on my hands and my eyes hurt,
And I know so little about cleaning a ship
That I would rather clean an island.
There one knows what one is about—sponge those palm trees, sweep up
    the sand a little, polish those coconuts;
Then take a rest for a while and it's time to trim the grass as well as
    separate it from each other where gummy substances have made
    individual blades stick together, forming an ugly bunch;
And then take the dead bark off the trees, and perfume these islands a bit
    with a song. . . . That's easy—but a battleship!
Where does one begin and how does one do? to batten the hatches? I
    would rather clean a million palm trees.

Now here comes an offer of a job for setting up a levee
In Mississippi. No thanks. Here it says *Rape or Worse.* I think they must
    want me to publicize this book.
On the jacket it says "Published in Boothbay Harbor, Maine"—what a
    funny place to publish a book!
I suppose it is some provincial publishing house
Whose provincial pages emit the odor of sails
And the freshness of the sea
Breeze. . . . But publicity!

The only thing I could publicize well would be my tooth,
Which I could say came with my mouth and in a most engaging
    manner
With my whole self, my body and including my mind,

Spirits, emotions, spiritual essences, emotional substances, poetry, dreams,
   and lords
Of my life, everything, all embraceleted with my tooth
In a way that makes one wish to open the windows and scream "Hi!" to
   the heavens,
And "Oh, come and take me away before I die in a minute!"

It is possible that the dentist is smiling, that he dreams of extraction
Because he believes that the physical tooth and the spiritual tooth are
   one.

Here is another letter, this one from a textbook advertiser;
He wants me to advertise a book on chopping down trees.
But how could I? I love trees! and I haven't the slightest sympathy with
   chopping them down, even though I know
We need their products for wood-fires, some houses, and maple syrup—
Still I like trees better
In their standing condition, when they sway at the beginning of
   evening . . .
And thank you for the pile of driftwood.
Am I wanted at the sea?

And thank you for the chance to run a small hotel
In an elephant stopover in Zambezi,
But I do not know how to take care of guests, certainly they would all
   leave soon
After seeing blue lights out the windows and rust on their iron beds—
   I'd rather own a bird-house in Jamaica:
Those people come in, the birds, they do not care how things are kept
   up . . .
It's true that Zambezi proprietorship would be exciting, with people
   getting off elephants and coming into my hotel,
But as tempting as it is I cannot agree.
And thank you for this offer of the post of referee
For the Danish wrestling championship—I simply do not feel
   qualified . . .

But the fresh spring air has been swabbing my mental decks
Until, although prepared for fight, still I sleep on land.
Thank you for the ostriches. I have not yet had time to pluck them,
But I am sure they will be delicious, adorning my plate at sunset,
My tremendous plate, and the plate
Of the offers to all my days. But I cannot fasten my exhilaration to the
    sun.

And thank you for the evening of the night on which I fell off my
    horse in the shadows. That was really useful.

Lunch

The lanternslides grinding out B-flat minor
Chords to the ears of the deaf youngster who sprays in Hicksville
The sides of a car with the dream-splitting paint
Of pianos (he dreamt of one day cutting the Conservatory
In two with his talent), these lanternslides, I say,
They are— The old woman hesitated. A lifesaver was shoved down her
    throat; then she continued:
They are some very good lanternslides in that bunch. Then she fainted
And we revived her with flowers. She smiled sleepily at the sun.
He is my own boy, she said, with her glass hand falling through the
    sparkling red America of lunch.

That old boilermaker she has in her back yard,
Olaf said, used to be her sweetheart years back.
One day, though, a train passed, and pressed her hard,
And she deserted life and love for liberty.
We carried Olaf softly into the back yard
And laid him down with his head under the steamroller.
Then Jill took the wheel and I tinkered with the engine,
Till we rolled him under, rolled him under the earth.
When people ask us what's in our back yard
Now, we don't like to tell them, Jill says, laying her silver bandannaed
    head on my greened bronze shoulder.
Then we both dazzle ourselves with the red whiteness of lunch.

That old woman named Tessie Runn
Had a tramp boyfriend who toasted a bun.
They went to Florida, but Maxine Schweitzer was hard of
Hearing and the day afterwards the judge adjourned the trial.
When it finally came for judgment to come up
Of delicious courtyards near the Pantheon,
At last we had to let them speak, the children whom flowers had made
    statues
For the rivers of water which came from their funnel;
And we stood there in the middle of existence
Dazzled by the white paraffin of lunch.

Music in Paris and water coming out from the flannel
Of the purist person galloping down the Madeleine
Toward a certain wafer. Hey! just a minute! the sunlight is being rifled
By the green architecture of the flowers. But the boulevard turned a big
    blue deaf ear
Of cinema placards to the detonated traveler. He had forgotten the blue
    defilade of lunch!

Genoa! a stone's throw from Acapulco
If an engine were built strong enough,
And down where the hulls and scungilli,
Glisteningly unconscious, agree,
I throw a game of shoes with Horace Sturnbul
And forget to eat lunch.

O launch, lunch, you dazzling hoary tunnel
To paradise!
Do you see that snowman tackled over there
By summer and the sea? A boardwalk went to Istanbul
And back under his left eye. We saw the Moslems praying
In Rhodes. One had a red fez, another had a black cap.
And in the extended heat of afternoon,
As an ice-cold gradual sweat covered my whole body,
I realized, and the carpet swam like a red world at my feet
In which nothing was green, and the Moslems went on praying,
That we had missed lunch, and a perpetual torrent roared into the sea
Of my understanding. An old woman gave us bread and rolls on the
    street.

The dancing wagon has come! here is the dancing wagon!
Come up and get lessons—here is lemonade and grammar!
Here is drugstore and cowboy—all that is America—plus sex, perfumes,
    and shimmers—all the Old World;
Come and get it—and here is your reading matter
For twenty-nine centuries, and here finally is lunch—
To be served in the green defilade under the roaring tower
Where Portugal meets Spain inside a flowered madeleine.

My ginger dress has nothing on, but yours
Has on a picture of Queen Anne Boleyn
Surrounded by her courtiers eating lunch
And on the back a one of Henry the Eighth
Summoning all his courtiers in for lunch.

And the lunchboat has arrived
From Spain.
Everyone getting sick is on it;
The bold people and the sadists are on it;
I am glad I am not on it,
I am having a big claw of garlic for lunch—
But it plucks me up in the air,
And there, above the ship, on a cloud
I see the angels eating lunch.
One has a beard, another a moustache,
And one has some mustard smeared on his ears.
A couple of them ask me if I want to go to Honolulu,
And I accept—it's all right—
Another time zone: we'll be able to have lunch.
They are very beautiful and transparent,
My two traveling companions,
And they will go very well with Hawaii
I realize as we land there,
That dazzling red whiteness—it is our desire . . .
For whom? The angels of lunch.

On I sat over a glass of red wine
And you came out dressed in a paper cup.
An ant-fly was eating hay-mire in the chair-rafters
And large white birds flew in and dropped edible animals to the ground.
If they had been gulls it would have been garbage
Or fish. We have to be fair to the animal kingdom,
But if I do not wish to be fair, if I wish to eat lunch
Undisturbed—? The light of day shines down. The world continues.

We stood in the little hutment in Biarritz

Waiting for lunch, and your hand clasped mine
And I felt it was sweaty;
And then lunch was served,
Like the bouquet of an enchantress.
Oh the green whites and red yellows
And purple whites of lunch!

The bachelor eats his lunch,
The married man eats his lunch,
And old Uncle Joris belches
The seascape in which a child appears
Eating a watermelon and holding a straw hat.
He moves his lips as if to speak
But only sea air emanates from this childish beak.
It is the moment of sorrows,
And on the shores of history,
Which stretch in both directions, there are no happy tomorrows.
But Uncle Joris holds his apple up and begins to speak
To the child. Red waves fan my universe with the green macaw of
    lunch.

This street is deserted;
I think my eyes are empty;
Let us leave
Quickly.
Day bangs on the door and is gone.

Then they picked him up and carried him away from that company.
When he awoke he was in the fire department, and sleepy but not tired.
They gave him a hoseful of blue Spain to eat for lunch,
And Portugal was waiting for him at the door, like a rainstorm of
    evening raspberries.

It is time to give lunch to my throat and not my chest.
What? either the sting ray has eaten my lunch
Or else—and she searches the sky for something else;
But I am far away, seeming blue-eyed, empirical . . .

Let us give lunch to the lunch—
But how shall we do it?
The headwaiters expand and confer;
Will little pieces of cardboard box do it?
And what about silver and gold pellets?
The headwaiters expand and confer:
And what if the lunch should refuse to eat anything at all?
Why then we'd say be damned to it,
And the red doorway would open on a green railway
And the lunch would be put in a blue car
And it would go away to Whippoorwill Valley
Where it would meet and marry Samuel Dogfoot, and bring forth seven
    offspring,
All of whom would be half human, half lunch;
And when we saw them, sometimes, in the gloaming,
We would take off our mining hats and whistle Tweet twee-oo,
With watering mouths staring at the girls in pink organdy frocks,
Not realizing they really were half edible,
And we would die still without knowing it;
So to prevent anything happening that terrible
Let's give everybody we see and like a good hard bite right now,
To see what they are, because it's time for lunch!

Taking a Walk with You

My misunderstandings: for years I thought "muso bello" meant "Bell
     Muse," I thought it was a kind of
Extra reward on the slotmachine of my shyness in the snow when
February was only a bouncing ball before the Hospital of the Two
     Sisters of the Last
Hamburger Before I Go to Sleep. I thought Axel's Castle was a garage;
And I had beautiful dreams about it, too—sensual, mysterious
     mechanisms; horns honking, wheels turning . . .
My misunderstandings were:
1) thinking Pinocchio could really change from a puppet into a real boy,
     and back again!
2) thinking it depended on whether he was good or bad!
3) identifying him with myself!
4) and therefore every time I was bad being afraid I would turn into
     wood . . .
5) I misunderstood childhood. I usually liked the age I was. However,
     now I regard twenty-nine as an optimum age (for me).
6) I disliked Shelley between twenty and twenty-five.
All of these things I suppose are understandable, but
When you were wearing your bodice I did not understand that you had
     nothing on beneath it;
When my father turned the corner I misunderstood the light very much
On Fifty-fifth Street; and I misunderstood (like an old Chinese
     restaurant) what he was doing there.
I misunderstood generally Oklahoma and Arkansas, though I think I
     understand New Mexico;
I understand the Painted Desert, cowboy hats, and vast spaces; I do
Not understand hillbilly life—I am sure I misunderstand it.
I did not understand that you had nothing on beneath your bodice
Nor, had I understood this, would I have understood what it meant;
     even now I
(Merry Christmas! Here, Father, take your package) misunderstand it!
Merry Christmas, Uncle Leon! yes, here is your package too.

I misunderstand Renaissance life; I misunderstand:
The Renaissance;
Ancient China;

The Middle Atlantic States and what they are like;
The tubes of London and what they mean;
Titian, Michelangelo, Vermeer;
The origins of words;
What others are talking about;
Music from the beginnings to the present time;
Laughter; and tears, even more so;
Value (economic and esthetic);
Snow (and weather in the country);
The meaning of the symbols and myths of Christmas.
I misunderstand you,
I misunderstand the day we walked down the street together for ten
    hours—
Where were we going? I had thought we were going somewhere. I
    believe I misunderstand many of the places we passed and things you
    said . . .
I misunderstand "Sons of Burgundy,"
I misunderstand that you had nothing painted beneath your bodice,
I misunderstand "Notification of Arrival or Departure to Be Eradicated
    Before Affection of Deceased Tenant."
I understand that
The smoke and the clouds are both a part of the day, but

I misunderstand the words "After Departure,"
I misunderstand nothingness;
I misunderstand the attitude of people in pharmacies, on the decks of
    ships, in my bedroom, amid the pine needles, on mountains of cotton,
    everywhere—
When they say paralytic I hear parasite, and when they say coffee I
    think music . . .
What is wrong with me from head to toe
That I misinterpret everything I hear? I misunderstand:
French: often;
Italian: sometimes, almost always—for example, if someone says,
    "Fortunate ones!" I am likely to think he is referring to the fountain
    with blue and red water (I am likely to make this mistake also in
    English).

I misunderstand Greek entirely;
I find ancient Greece very hard to understand: I probably misunderstand
  it;
I misunderstand spoken German about 98% of the time, like the
  cathedral in the middle of a town;
I misunderstand "Beautiful Adventures"; I also think I probably
  misunderstand *La Nausée* by Jean-Paul Sartre . . .
I probably misunderstand misunderstanding itself—I misunderstand the
  Via Margutta in Rome, or Via della Vite, no matter what street, all
  of them.
I misunderstand wood in the sense of its relationship to the tree; I
  misunderstand people who take one attitude or another about it . . .
Spring I would like to say I understand, but I most probably don't—
  autumn, winter, and summer are all in the same boat
(Ruined ancient cities by the sea).

I misunderstand *vacation* and *umbrella,*
I misunderstand *motion* and *weekly*
(Though I think I understand "Daytime Pissarros"
And the octagon—I do not understand the public garden) . . .

Oh I am sure there is a use for all of them, but what is it?
My misunderstandings confuse Rome and Ireland, and can you
Bring that beautiful sex to bear upon it?
I misunderstand what I am saying, though not to you;
I misunderstand a large boat: that is a ship.
What you are feeling for me I misunderstand totally; I think I
  misunderstand the very possibilities of feeling,
Especially here in Rome, where I somehow think I am.
I see the sky, and sails.
(I misunderstand the mustard and the bottle)
Oh that we could go sailing in that sky!

What tune came with the refreshments?
I am unable to comprehend why they were playing off key.
Is it because they wanted us to jump over the cliff
Or was one of them a bad or untrained musician

Or the whole lot of them?
At any rate
San Giovanni in Laterano
Also resisted my questioning
And turned a deaf blue dome to me
Far too successfully.
I cannot understand why you walk forwards and backwards with me.
I think it is because you want to try out your shoes for their toes.
It is Causation that is my greatest problem
And after that the really attentive study of millions of details.

I love you, but it is difficult to stop writing.
As a flea could write the Divine Comedy of a water jug. Now Irish
    mists close in upon us.
Peat sails through the air, and greenness becomes bright. Are you the
    ocean or the island? Am I on Irish soil, or are your waves covering
    me?
St. Peter's bells are ringing: "Earthquake, inundation, and sleep to the
    understanding!"
(American Express! flower vendors! your beautiful straight nose! that
    delightful trattoria in Santa Maria in Trastevere!)
Let us have supper at Santa Maria in Trastevere
Where by an absolute and total misunderstanding (but not fatal) I once
    ate before I met you.
I am probably misinterpreting your answer, since I hear nothing, and I
    believe I am alone.

The Railway Stationery

The railway stationery lay upon
The desk of the railway clerk, from where he could see
The springtime and the tracks. Engraved upon
Each page was an inch-and-a-half-high T
And after that an H and then an E
And then, slightly below it to the right,
There was COLUMBUS RAILWAY COMPANY
In darker ink as the above was light.
The print was blue. And just beneath it all
There was an etching—not in blue, but black—
Of a real railway engine half-an-inch tall
Which, if you turned the paper on its back,
You could see showing through, as if it ran
To one edge of the sheet then back again.

To one edge of the sheet then back again!
The springtime comes while we're still drenched in snow
And, whistling now, snow-spotted Number Ten
Comes up the track and stops, and we must go
Outside to get its cargo, with our hands
Cold as the steel they touch. Inside once more
Once we have shut the splintery wooden door
Of the railway shack, the stationery demands
Some further notice. For the first time the light,
Reflected from the snow by the bright spring sun,
Shows that the engine wheel upon the right
Is slightly darker than the left-side one
And slightly lighter than the one in the center,
Which may have been an error of the printer.

Shuffling through many sheets of it to establish
Whether this difference is consistent will
Prove that it is not. Probably over-lavish
At the beginning with the ink, he still
(The printer) had the presence of mind to change
His operating process when he noticed
That on the wheels the ink had come out strange.

Because the windows of the shack are latticed
The light that falls upon the stationery
Is often interrupted by straight lines
Which shade the etching. Now the words "Dear Mary"
Appear below the engine on one sheet
Followed by a number of other conventional signs,
Among which are "our love," "one kiss," and "sweet."

The clerk then signs his name—his name is Johnson,
But all he signs is Bill, with a large B
Which overflows its boundaries like a Ronson
With too much fluid in it, which you see
Often, and it can burn you, though the *i*
Was very small and had a tiny dot.
The *l*'s were different—the first was high,
The second fairly low. And there was a spot
Of ink at the end of the signature which served
To emphasize that the letter was complete.
On the whole, one could say his writing swerved
More than the average, although it was neat.
He'd used a blue-black ink, a standing pen,
Which now he stuck back in its stand again.

Smiling and sighing, he opened up a drawer
And took an envelope out, which then he sealed
After he'd read the letter three times more
And folded it and put it in. A field
Covered with snow, untouched by man, is what
The envelope resembled, till he placed
A square with perforated edges that
Pictured a white-haired President, who faced
The viewer, in its corner, where it stuck
After he'd kissed its back and held it hard
Against the envelope. Now came the truck
Of the postman "Hello, Jim." "Hello there, Bill."
"I've got this—can you take it?" "Sure, I will!"

Now the snow fell down gently from the sky.
Strange wonder—snow in spring! Bill walked into
The shack again and wrote the letter *I*
Idly upon a sheet of paper. New
Ideas for writing Mary filled his mind,
But he resisted—there was work to do.
For in the distance he could hear the grind
Of the Seventy-Eight, whose engine was half blue;
So, putting on a cap, he went outside
On the tracks side, to wait for it to come.
It was the Seventy-Eight which now supplied
The city with most of its produce, although some
Came in by truck and some was grown in town.
Now it screams closer, and he flags it down.

The Departure from Hydra

As I was walking home just now, from seeing
Margaret and Norris off (though Peter,
An Englishman whom Norris had met yesterday,
Went back to change his clothes, and missed the boat)
As I came home along the little street
Without a name on which the only theatre,
The movie theatre, on Hydra is,
Called "The Gardenia" or just plain "Gardenia,"
The street which they today are tearing up
And carrying new stones in to replace
The ones they're tearing up, though it may be
They are the same stones, put in different order
Or in a different way, as I was walking,
With the heat of the day just over, at five-thirty,
I felt quite good, but then felt an awareness
Of something in my legs that might be painful
And then of some slight tension in my jaws
And slight pains in my head; instead of despairing
And giving all thought of pleasure up, I felt
That if I could write down all that I felt
As I came walking there, that that would be
A pleasure also, and with solidity.
I passed a mule—some men were loading up
His fellow-mule with packets—and I stared
At his wide eyes and his long hard flat nose
Or face, at which he turned away his eyes
And stamped his right hoof nervously. I felt
Guilty, a member of a higher species
Deliberately using my power against
A natural inferior because
Really I was afraid that he might kick
When I came past; but when he seemed upset
Then I felt guilty. Then I looked ahead
And saw a view of houses on the hill,
Particularly noticing one red one
And thinking, Yes, that is a part of what
I feel, of the variety of this walk;

Then my mind blurred somewhat, I turned and came
Down this small narrow alley to my home.
As I came in, reviewing the ideas
Which had occurred to me throughout my walk,
It suddenly came to me that maybe Peter
Had missed the Athens boat deliberately;
After all, Margaret was not sure that she
Wanted to accompany him and Norris
On a walking trip on Poros, and Norris had said
He wanted to stay with Margaret, so that Peter
Was disappointed, since he and Norris had planned
That very morning to take such a walking trip,
And he, Peter, had been the most excited
Of all, about it. But now since Margaret and Norris
Were going into Athens, what was there for Peter
To do, why should he take the boat at all,
Even though he'd planned to, to stop at Poros?
Except, of course, to act on some marginal chance
That Norris might get off with him and walk,
Or on the strength of previous expectations,
Emotional impetus lingering. If not,
Perhaps his going to change was just an excuse
To avoid an actual confrontation with Norris
In which he would have to say, No, I'm not going
Unless you'll come on the walking trip!" but he knew,
Peter, that Norris wanted to stay with Margaret
And that therefore speaking to him would only result
In a little pain and confusion, since both were quite drunk,
Having planned their trip to Poros over beer all morning;
And also, of course, it might result in his getting,
In spite of himself, on the boat, by the talk confused
And not thinking clearly (whereas if he walked away
He had only, really, to wait till the boat had left—
Then he could come back down and think it over,
Surely to find he didn't regret too much
Not getting the boat, because after all the reason
He'd wanted to take the boat had long been gone).

For a human situation often leads
People to do things that they don't desire
At all, but they find that what they did desire
Has somehow led them to this situation
In which not to do that which is proposed
Seems inconsistent, hostile, or insane,
Though much more often very unfriendly; then too
Sometimes it chiefly is a lack of time
To explain how things have changed that leads one, waving
One's hands, aboard a ship that bodes one ill.
To walk away as Peter did is one way
Of avoiding such situations—another way
Is never to deceive or have high hopes
For foolish things; to be straight with oneself,
With one's own body, nature, and society,
To cast off everything that is not clear
And definite, and move toward one desire
After another, with no afterthoughts.
Living in this way one avoids the sudden
Transports of excitement Peter felt
When Norris mentioned a Poros walking tour.
For surely if Peter's natural desires
Had all been satisfied, if his life were running
Smoothly sexually, and if his health
Were excellent and his work going well,
He scarcely would have gotten so excited
At the mere thought of walking around Poros;
This sort of thing, however, often happens
To people from Northern countries, not just Peter,
And perhaps if one is English, Norse, or Swedish,
Danish, Finnish, Swiss, or North American,
One cannot avoid a certain amount of tension,
A certain quavering in the hand which reaches
For a ripe peach or the shoulder of a girl,
One whom, as one walks back from going swimming,
One thinks that one could eat, she's so delicious,
But only thinks it for a little while

(This thought itself is such a Northern one!
A Southerner would think about a place
Where he could go and jump on top of her)—
In any case, then, Northerners find it hard
To avoid such sudden excitements, but the English,
And especially the upper class, are worst of all,
Because besides their climate that's oppressed them
There's also been a restrictive upbringing,
Manners around the house perhaps too severe
For children—I am speaking of those English
Who escape from "class" and become bright or artistic,
The ones one sees on places like this island.
(These sudden outbursts of enthusiasm, of course,
Are often much admired by other people,
Particularly some not very smart ones,
Who think however they're very sensitive
And what they most admire is "vitality"
Which they think things like outbursts are a sign of,
And they can bore you far into the night
With telling you how wonderful some Dane
Or Norsky is, when you could be asleep
Dreaming of satisfying your desires
With persons who are always very warm,
Tender, and exciting—but, awake!
They're talking still, and though your sickly smile
Gets sicklier every moment, they go on:
"Hans suddenly got the idea to
Inundate Denmark. He is wonderful!"
"Oh, marvelous! Where does one go to meet him?"
"I'll give you his address. He has a farm
Where he stays in the summer; he loves animals,
But sometimes when he drinks a lot he beats them
And says that he can understand their language."
"How marvelous!" "And here's his city address:
Beschtungen aber Bass Gehundenweiss
996." "Goodnight." But Peter is
Not an exaggerated case like that,

And not a nagging bore who talks of such
People, but he has "outbursts" all the same.
It is true, in a sense these outbursts are
Difficult to discriminate from real
Vitality, which everyone esteems
These days because of man's oppressed position
In modern society, which saps his strength
And makes him want to do what everyone else does,
Whereas some man who says, "Let's pitch the glasses
Against the lamppost" is likely to be praised
By some low-IQ person who is there
As being really vital, ah he's wonderful.
Vitality, however, usually
Appeals to an answering vital force in others
And brings about making love or great events,
Or it at least gives pleasure—I can't judge
Vitality in any way but the way
It gives me pleasure, for if I do not get
Pleasure from life, of which vitality
Is just the liquid form, then what am I
And who cares what I say? I for one don't.
Therefore I judge vitality that way.)
But Peter, after having this idea
Of a walking trip on Poros, must have felt
That in walking around in the sun all day on an island
About which he knew nothing, there might come
Some insight to him or some relaxation,
Some feeling the way an Italian feels all the time,
Or perhaps not, perhaps he never does;
Peter at any rate was probably not
Conscious of an Italian at the time
He thought with pleasure about the walk on Poros,
But there he was, faced with Norris and Margaret
An hour before the boat came in, and Norris
Was saying "Maybe not." One mistake of Peter,
Or, rather, difficulty, a common one
In such enthusiasms, is that since

One's enthusiasm is motivated by submerged
Feelings and so its object isn't clear
To anyone, it is most likely that
Though they respond excitedly at first,
Partly because excitement is so communicable,
Others, when they think over what you've planned,
Will see it in a greyer light, unless of course
They have the same neuroses that you have,
In which case a whole lifetime might be built
Upon one of these outbursts. Norris, probably,
In drinking with Peter, wanted more than anything
To be agreeable, whereas Peter wanted
To "do" something unusual, not necessarily
Pleasing to Norris, not necessarily displeasing;
Norris, I should imagine, then, once he
Was out of Peter's company, since he'd known him
A very short time, was lacking the chief impulse
That motivated him when he agreed
To take a tour with Peter; therefore Margaret,
Speaking to Norris when he was alone
And saying she did not want to take the trip,
Found he immediately agreed with her,
Expressed some doubts at least, and said all right,
The trip was off then, he'd explain to Peter;
Peter, of course, was very surprised by this,
But still he must have been used to it because
The way that Norris and Margaret acted was based
On laws of human conduct which endure;
And since that outburst surely was not his first,
Peter was probably accustomed to
That sort of outcome of his impulses
And said to himself, "Ah, they don't understand,"
But probably knew inside that there was something
Seriously the matter with him. So when he left
The table and said, "I'm going to get my things,"
It was with a certain tension that he left,
Indicative of the fact he'd not come back,

And of the fact that he knew he would not avoid
Self-doubts because he avoided the useless boat trip;
Of course he wouldn't think he should have gone
But wonder why things had been the way they were.
It was these deeper worries in his mind,
I think, that kept him from leaving even sooner
With the same excuse, rather than a hope that Norris
Would change his mind again. Deep thoughts make helpless
Men for small undertakings. Well, perhaps
The last is speculation, but the rest
Seems surely true. I smiled, and closed the door.

from

The
Pleasures
of Peace

West Wind

It's the ocean of western steel
Bugles that makes me want to listen
To the parting of the trees
Like intemperate smiles, in a
Storm coat evangelistically ground
Out of spun glass and silver threads
When stars are in my head, and we
Are apart and together, friend of my youth
Whom I've so recently met—a fragment of the universe
In our coats, a believable doubling
Of the fresh currents of doubt and
Thought! a winter climate
Found in the Southern Hemisphere and where
I am who offers you to wear,
And in this storm, along the tooth of the street,
The intemperate climate of this double frame of the universe.

Hearing

Hear the beautiful tinny voices of the trumpets
Beside the rushing sound of the great blue waterfall;
See the guns fire, then hear the leaves drop to the ground;
Lie back in your chair—and now there is the clatter of pennies!
The familiar scraping noise of the chair feet on the ground,
As if a worm had grown six feet tall! And here is the worm,
And hear his softly scraping noise at the forest gate.
In the Bourse the diamonds clink and clank against each other,
And the violet airplane speaks to the farmland with its buzz
From high in the air, but you hear the slice
Of shears and watch the happy gardener's face whiten
As he hears the final throbs of his failing heart.
All is not stillness—far from it. The tinny
Trumpets renew their song among the eglantine's
Too speciously gracious brilliance, and a hen drops
An egg, with infinite gentleness, into the straw.

Who is this young man with the tremendous French horn in the garden
With a lady in lilac bending her head to catch each note
That flows, serene and unbidden, from the silvery throat?
I think they are strangers here. Stones fall in the pool.
She smiles, she is very witty, she bends too far, and now we hear
The sound of her lilac dress ripping in the soft summer air.
For it is summer! Hear the cool rush of the stream and the heavy black
Vocalism of leaves in the wind. A note then comes, arises
In the air, it is a glass in which a few warm drops of rain
Make music; there are roars and meows, turkeys and spaniels
Come running to the great piano, which, covered with pearls,
Gives extra, clinking sounds to your delighted ears;
And the dogs bark, and there is the little thrilled silence of snails. . . .
Above all else you hear the daisies being torn apart
By tremendous bumblebees who have come here from another
    Department!
"Wisteria tapping the house, so comes your blood. . . ."

Now rain, now this earth streams with water!
Hear the tooting of Triton among the clouds

And on the earth! See the trumpets of heaven floating toward us
Blaring among the wet masses of citron and vermilion wings!
They play "Put down the cushion on the chair,
Put down the cushion on the chair, put down
The cushion, put it down, put the cushion down on the chair,
Ra ta ta. . . ." The young man's French horn is wet, it makes a different
  noise,
The girl turns her face toward him and he hears strings (it is another
  tear in her dress!).
In the kitchen the sound of raspberries being mashed in the cream
Reminds you of your childhood and all the fantasies you had then!
In the highest part of an oak tree is a blue bird
Trilling. A drying friend reads *Orlando Furioso*
Sitting on a beach chair; then you hear awnings being stretched out!
A basso sings, and a soprano answers him.
Then there is thunder in a clear blue sky,
And, from the earth, a sigh: "This song is finished."

Poem

The thing
To do
Is organize
The sea
So boats will
Automatically float
To their destinations.
Ah, the Greeks
Thought of that!
Well, what if
They
Did? We have no
Gods
Of the winds!
And therefore
Must use
Science!

Ma Provence

En ma Provence le blé est toujours vert
Et les filles sont jolies
Elles ne meurent pas elles vous aiment à la folie—en ma Provence.

Bills break the breakfast teacups and the sun
Shines darkly over the bill-ware
She writes it out in enervating prose
"In my Provence, my rose."

Sleeping with Women

Caruso: a voice.
Naples: sleeping with women.
Women: sleeping in the dark.
Voices: a music.
Pompeii: a ruin.
Pompeii: sleeping with women.
Men sleeping with women, women sleeping with women, sheep sleeping
   with women, everything sleeping with women.
The guard: asking you for a light.
Women: asleep.
Yourself: asleep.
Everything south of Naples: asleep and sleeping with them.
Sleeping with women: as in the poems of Pascoli.
Sleeping with women: as in the rain, as in the snow.
Sleeping with women: by starlight, as if we were angels, sleeping on the
   train,
On the starry foam, asleep and sleeping with them—sleeping with
   women.
Mediterranean: a voice.
Mediterranean: a sea. Asleep and sleeping.
Streetcar in Oslo, sleeping with women, Toonerville Trolley
In Stockholm asleep and sleeping with them, in Skansen
Alone, alone with women,
The rain sleeping with women, the brain of the dog-eyed genius
Alone, sleeping with women, all he has wanted,
The dog-eyed fearless man.
Sleeping with them: as in *The Perils of Pauline*
Asleep with them: as in Tosca
Sleeping with women and causing all that trouble
As in Roumania, as in Yugoslavia
Asleep and sleeping with them
Anti-Semitic, and sleeping with women,
Pro-canary, Rashomon, Shakespeare, tonight, sleeping with women
A big guy sleeping with women
A black seacoast's sleeve, asleep with them
And sleeping with women, and sleeping with them
The Greek islands sleeping with women

The muddy sky, asleep and sleeping with them.
Sleeping with women, as in a scholarly design
Sleeping with women, as if green polarity were a line
Into the sea, sleeping with women
As if wolverines, in a street line, as if sheep harbors
Could come alive from sleeping with women, wolverines
Greek islands sleeping with women, Nassos, Naxos, Kos,
Asleep with women, Mykonos, miotis,
And myositis, sleeping with women, blue-eyed
Red-eyed, green-eyed, yellow reputed, white-eyed women
Asleep and sleeping with them, blue, sleeping with women
As in love, as at sea, the rabbi, asleep and sleeping with them
As if that could be, the stones, the restaurant, asleep and sleeping with
    them,
Sleeping with women, as if they were knee
Arm and thigh asleep and sleeping with them, sleeping with women.
And the iris peg of the sea
Sleeping with women
And the diet pill of the tree
Sleeping with women
And the apology the goon the candlelight
The groan: asking you for the night, sleeping with women
Asleep and sleeping with them, the green tree
The iris, the swan: the building with its mouth open
Asleep with women, awake with man,
The sunlight, asleep and sleeping with them, the moving gong
The abacus, the crab, asleep and sleeping with them
And moving, and the moving van, in London, asleep with women
And intentions, inventions for sleeping with them
Lands sleeping with women, ants sleeping with women, Italo-Greek or
    Anglo-French orchestras
Asleep with women, asleep and sleeping with them,
The foam and the sleet, asleep and sleeping with them,
The schoolboy's poem, the crippled leg
Asleep and sleeping with them, sleeping with women
Sleeping with women, as if you were a purist
Asleep and sleeping with them.

Sleeping with women: there is no known form for the future
Of this undreamed-of view: sleeping with a chorus
Of highly tuned women, asleep and sleeping with them.
Bees, sleeping with women
And tourists, sleeping with them
Soap, sleeping with women; beds, sleeping with women
The universe: a choice
The headline: a voice, sleeping with women
At dawn, sleeping with women, asleep and sleeping with them.
Sleeping with women: a choice, as of a mule
As of an island, asleep or sleeping with them, as of a Russia,
As of an island, as of a drum: a choice of views: asleep and sleeping
    with them, as of high noon, as of a choice, as of variety, as of the
    sunlight, red student, asleep and sleeping with them,
As with an orchid, as with an oriole, at school, sleeping with women,
    and you are the one
The one sleeping with women, in Mexico, sleeping with women
The ghost land, the vectors, sleeping with women
The motel man, the viaduct, the sun
The universe: a question
The moat: a cathexis
What have we done? On Rhodes, man
On Samos, dog
Sleeping with women
In the rain and in the sun
The dog has a red eye, it is November
Asleep and sleeping with them, sleeping with women
This June: a boy
October: sleeping with women
The motto: a sign; the bridge: a definition.
To the goat: destroy; to the rain: be a settee.
O rain of joy: sleeping with women, asleep and sleeping with them.
Volcano, Naples, Caruso, asleep and sleeping, asleep and sleeping with
    them
The window, the windrow, the hedgerow, irretrievable blue,
Sleeping with women, the haymow, asleep and sleeping with them, the
    canal

Asleep and sleeping with them, the eagle's feather, the dock's weather,
    and the glue:
Sleeping with you; asleep and sleeping with you: sleeping with women.
Sleeping with women, charming aspirin, as in the rain, as in the snow,
Asleep and sleeping with you: as if the crossbow, as of the moonlight
Sleeping with women: as if the tractate, as if d'Annunzio
Asleep and sleeping with you, asleep with women
Asleep and sleeping with you, asleep with women, asleep and sleeping
    with you, sleeping with women
As if the sun, as of Venice and the Middle Ages' "true
Renaissance had just barely walked by the yucca
Forest" asleep and sleeping with you
In China, on parade, sleeping with women
And in the sun, asleep and sleeping with you, sleeping with women,
Asleep with women, the docks, the alley, and the prude
Sleeping with women, asleep with them.
The dune god: sleeping with women
The dove: asleep and sleeping with them
Dials sleeping with women; cybernetic tiles asleep and sleeping with
    them
Naples: sleeping with women; the short of breath
Asleep and sleeping with you, sleeping with women
As if I were you—moon idealism
Sleeping with women, pieces of stageboard, sleeping with women
The silent bus ride, sleeping with you.
The chore: sleeping with women
The force of a disaster: sleeping with you
The organ grinder's daughter: asleep with bitumen, sunshine, sleeping
    with women,
Sleeping with women: in Greece, in China, in Italy, sleeping with blue
Red green orange and white women, sleeping with two
Three four and five women, sleeping on the outside
And on the inside of women, a violin, like a vista, women, sleeping
    with women
In the month of May, in June, in July
Sleeping with women, "I watched my life go by" sleeping with women
A door of pine, a stormfilled valentine asleep and sleeping with them

"This Sunday heart of mine" profoundly dormoozed with them
They running and laughing, asleep and sleeping with them
"This idle heart of mine" insanely "shlamoozed" asleep and sleeping with
    them,
They running in laughter
To the nearest time, oh doors of eternity
Oh young women's doors of my own time! sleeping with women
Asleep and sleeping with them, all Naples asleep and sleeping with them,
Venice sleeping with women, Burgos sleeping with women, Lausanne
    sleeping with women, hail depth-divers
Sleeping with women, and there is the bonfire of Crete
Catching divorce in its fingers, purple sleeping with women
And the red lights of dawn, have you ever seen them, green ports
    sleeping with women, acrobats and pawns,
You had not known it ere I told it you asleep with women
The Via Appia Antica asleep with women, asleep and sleeping with them
All beautiful objects, each ugly object, the intelligent world,
The arena of the spirits, the dietetic whisky, the storms
Sleeping with women, asleep and sleeping with them,
Sleeping with women. And the churches in Antigua, sleeping with
    women
The stone: a vow
The Nereid: a promise—to sleep with women
The cold—a convention: sleeping with women
The carriage: sleeping with women
The time: sometimes
The certainty: now
The soapbox: sleeping with women
The time and again nubile and time, sleeping with women, and the time
    now
Asleep and sleeping with them, asleep and asleep, sleeping with women,
    asleep and sleeping with them, sleeping with women.

The Pleasures of Peace

Another ribald tale of the good times at Madame Lipsky's.
Giorgio Finogle had come in with an imitation of the latest Russian
poet,
The one who wrote the great "Complaint About the Peanut Farm"
which I read to you last year at Mrs. Riley's,
Do you remember? and then of course Giorgio had written this
imitation
So he came in with it. . . . Where was I and what was I saying?
The big beer parlor was filled with barmaids and men named Stuart
Who were all trying to buy a big red pitcher of beer for an artiste
named Alma Stuart
Whom each claimed as his very own because of the similarity in
names—
This in essence was Buddy's parody—Oh Giorgio, you idiot, Marian
Stuart snapped,
It all has something to do with me! But no, Giorgio replied,
Biting in a melancholy way the edge off a cigar-paper-patterned
envelope
In which he had been keeping the Poem for many days
Waiting to show it to his friends. And actually it's not a parody at all,
I just claimed it was, out of embarrassment. It's a poetic present for you
all,
All of whom I love! Is it capable to love more than one—I wonder!
Alma cried,
And we went out onto the bicycle-shaped dock where a malicious
swarm of mosquitoes
Were parlaying after having invaded the old beer parlor.
The men named Stuart were now involved in a fight to the death
But the nearer islands lay fair in the white night light.
Shall we embark toward them? I said, placing my hand upon one
exceedingly gentle
And fine. A picture of hairnets is being projected. Here
Comes someone with Alma Stuart! Is it real, this night? Or have we a
gentle fantasy?
The Russian poet appears. He seems to consider it real all right. He's
Quite angry. Where's the Capitalist fairy that put me down? he squirts

At our nomadic simplicity. "Complaint About the Peanut Farm" is a
    terrific poem. Yes,
In a way, yes. The Hairdresser of Night engulfs them all in foam.

"I love your work, *The Pleasures of Peace,*" the Professor said to me next
    day;
"I think it adequately encompasses the hysteria of our era
And puts certain people in their rightful place. Chapeau! Bravo!"
"You don't get it," I said. "I like all this. I called this poem
Pleasures of Peace because I'm not sure they will be lasting!
I wanted people to be able to see what these pleasures are
That they may come back to them." "But they are all so hysterical, so—
    so transitory,"
The critic replied. "I mean, how can you—what kind of pleasures are
    these?
They seem more like pains to me—if I may say what I mean."
"Well, I don't know, Professor," I said; "permanent joys
Have so far been denied this hysterical person. Though I confess
Far other joys I've had and will describe in time.
And then too there's the pleasure of *writing* these—perhaps to experience
    is not the same."
The Professor paused, lightly, upon the temple stair.
"I will mention you among the immortals, Ken," he said,
"Because you have the courage of what you believe.
But there I will never mention those sniveling rats
Who only claim to like these things because they're fashionable."
"Professor!" I cried, "My darling! my dream!" And she stripped, and I
    saw there
Creamy female marble, the waist and thighs of which I had always
    dreamed.
"Professor! Loved one! why the disguise?" "It was a test," she said,
"Of which you have now only passed the first portion.
You must write More, and More—"
"And be equally persuasive?" I questioned, but She
Had vanished through the Promontory door.

So now I must devote my days to The Pleasures of Peace—
To my contemporaries I'll leave the Horrors of War,

They can do them better than I—each poet shares only a portion
Of the vast Territory of Rhyme. Here in Peace shall I stake out
My temporal and permanent claim. But such silver as I find
I will give to the Universe—the gold I'll put in other poems.
Thus in time there'll be a mountain range of gold
Of considerable interest. Oh may you come back in time
And in my lifetime to see it, most perfect and most delectable reader!
We poets in our youth begin with fantasies,
But then at least we think they may be realities—
The poems we create in our age
Require your hand upon our shoulder, your eye on our page.

Here are listed all the Pleasures of Peace that there could possibly be.
Among them are the pleasures of Memory (which Delmore Schwartz
    celebrated), the pleasures of autonomy,
The pleasures of agoraphobia and the sudden release
Of the agoraphobic person from the identified marketplace, the pleasures
    of roving over you
And rolling over the beach, of being in a complicated car, of sleeping,
Of drawing ropes with you, of planning a deranged comic strip, of
    shifting knees
At the accelerator pump, of blasphemy, of cobra settlement in a
    dilapidated skin country
Without clops, and therefore every pleasure is also included; which, after
    these—

Chapter Thirty Seven.
On the Planisphere everyone was having a nut
When suddenly my Lulu appeared.
She was a big broad about six feet seven
And she had a red stone in her ear
Which was stringent in its beauty.
I demanded at once the removal of people from the lobby
So we could begin to down ABC tablets and start to feel funny
But Mordecai La Schlomp our Leader replied that we did not need any
That a person could feel good without any artificial means.

Oh the Pleasures of Peace are infinite and they cannot be counted—
One single piece of pink mint chewing gum contains more pleasures
Than the whole rude gallery of war! And the moon passes by
In an otherwise undistinguished lesson on the geography of this age
Which has had fifty-seven good lovers and ninety-six wars. By Giorgio
     Finogle.

It turns out that we're competing for the Peace Award,
Giorgio Finogle and I. We go into the hair parlor, the barber—
We get to talking about war and about peace.
The barber feels that we are really good people at heart
Even though his own views turn out to be conservative.
"I've read Finogle's piece, the part of it that was in *Smut*," he
Says, "and I liked it. Yours, Koch, I haven't yet seen,
But Alyne and Francie told me that you were the better poet."
"I don't know," I said. "Giorgio is pretty good." And Giorgio comes
     back from the bathroom
Now, with a grin on his face. "I've got an idea for my
Pleasures of Peace," he says; "I'm going to make it include
Each person in the universe discussing their own bag—
Translation, their main interest, and what they want to be—"
"You'll never finish it, Giorgio," I said. "At least I'll
Get started," he replied, and he ran out of the barbershop.

In the quiet night we take turns riding horseback and falling asleep.
Your breasts are more beautiful than a gold mine.
I think I'll become a professional man.
The reason we are up-to-date is we're some kind of freaks.
I don't know what to tell the old man
But he is concerned with two kinds of phenomena and I am interested
     in neither. What *are* you interested in?
Being some kind of freaks, I think. Let's go to Transylvania.
I don't understand your buddy all the time. Who?
The one with HANDLEBAR written across his head.
He's a good guy, he just doesn't see the difference between a man and a
     bike. If I love you
It's because you belong to and have a sublime tolerance
For such people. Yes, but in later life, I mean—

It is Present Life we've got to keep up on the screen,
Isn't it. Well yes, she said, but—
I am very happy that you are interested in it. The French poodle
    stopped being Irish entirely
And we are all out of the other breeds.
The society woman paused, daintily, upon the hotel stair.
No, I must have a poodle, said she; not an Irish setter
Would satisfy me in my mad passion for the poodle breeds!
As usual, returning to the bed
I find that you are inside it and sound asleep. I smile happily and look
    at your head.
It is regular-size and has beautiful blonde hair all around it.
Some is lying across the pillow. I touch it with my feet
Then leap out the window into the public square,
And I tune my guitar.

"O Mistress Mine, where are you roving?" That's my tune! roars
    Finogle, and he
Comes raging out of the *Beefsteak*—I was going to put that in MY
    Pleasures of Peace.
Oh normal comportment! even you too I shall include in the Pleasures
    of Peace,
And you, relative humidity five hundred and sixty-two degrees!
But what of you, poor sad glorious aqueduct
Of boorish ashes made by cigarettes smoked at the Cupcake
Award—And Sue Ellen Musgrove steps on one of my feet. "Hello!"
She says. "You're that famous COKE, aren't you,
That no one can drink? When are you going to give us your famous
    Iliad
That everyone's been talking of, I mean your Pleasures of Peace!"

Life changes as the universe changes, but the universe changes
More slowly, as bedevilments increase.
Sunlight comes through a clot for example
Which Zoo Man has thrown on the floor. It is the Night of the Painted
    Pajamas
And the Liberals are weeping for peace. The Conservatives are raging for
    it.

The Independents are staging a parade. And we are completely naked
Walking through the bedroom for peace. I have this friend who had
    myopia
So he always had to get very close to people
And girls thought he was trying to make out—
Why didn't he get glasses?—He was a Pacifist! The Moon shall
    overcome!

Outside in the bar yard the Grecians are screaming for peace
And the Alsatians, the Albanians, the Alesians, the Rubans, the Aleutians,
And the Iranians, all, all are screaming for peace.
They shall win it, their peace, because I am going to help them!
And he leaped out the window for peace!
Headline: GIORGIO FINOGLE,
NOTED POET, LAST NIGHT LEAPED OUT THE WINDOW
    FOR PEACE.
ASIDE FROM HEAD INJURIES HIS CONDITION IS REPORTED
    NORMAL.
But Giorgio never was normal! Oh the horrors of peace,
I mean of peace-fighting! But Giorgio is all right,
He is still completely himself. "I am going to throw this hospital
Bed out the window for peace," when we see him, he says.
And, "Well, I guess your poem will be getting way ahead of mine
    now," he says
Sadly, ripping up an envelope for peace and weakly holding out his
    hand
For my girl, Ellen, to stroke it; "I will no longer be the most famous
    poet
For peace. You will, and you know it." "But you jumped out the
Window, Finogle," I said, "and your deed shall live longer
In men's imaginations than any verse." But he looked at the sky
Through the window's beautiful eye and he said, "Kenneth, I have not
    written one word
Of my Poem for Peace for three weeks. I've struck a snarl
And that's why (I believe) I jumped out the
Window—pure poetic frustration. Now tell them all that, how
They'll despise me, oh sob sob—" "Giorgio," I said, trying to calm him
    down but laughing

So hard I could barely digest the dinner of imagination
In which your breasts were featured as on a Popeye card
When winter has lighted the lanterns and the falls are asleep
Waiting for next day's shards, "Giorgio," I said, "the pleasures—"
But hysteria transported us all.

When I awoke you were in a star-shaped muffin, I was in a loaf of
    bread
Shaped like a camera, and Giorgio was still in his hospital bed
But a huge baker loomed over us. One false moof and I die you! he
    said
In a murderous throaty voice and I believe in the yellow leaves, the
Orange, the red leaves of autumn, the tan leaves, and the promoted ones
Of green, of green and blue. Sometimes walking through an ordinary
    garden
You will see a bird, and the overcoat will fall from your
Shoulders, slightly, exposing one beautiful curve
On which sunbeams alighting forget to speak a single word
To their parent sun and are thus cut off
Without a heating unit, but need none being on your breast
Which I have re-christened "Loaves" for the beginning of this year
In which I hope the guns won't fire any more, the baker sang
To his baker lady, and then he had totally disappeared.
It looks as though everyone were going to be on our side!

And the flowers came out, and they were on our side,
Even the yellow little ones that grow beside your door
And the huge orange ones were bending to one side
As we walked past them, I looked into your blue eyes
And I said, "If we come out of this door
Any more, let it be to enter only this nervous paradise
Of peaceful living conditions, and if Giorgio is roped down
Let them untie him, so he can throw his hospital bed out the door
For all we need besides peace, which is considerable, but first we need
    that—"

Daredevil, Julian and Maddalo, and John L. Lewis
Are running down the stairways for peace, they are gathering the ice
And throwing it in buckets, they are raising purple parasols for peace

And on top of these old sunlight sings her song, "New lights, old lights
   again, blue lights for peace,
Red lights for the low, insulted parasol, and a few crutches thrown
   around for peace"—
Oh contentment is the key
To continuing exploration of the nations and their feet;
Therefore, andiamo—the footfall is waiting in the car
And peaceful are the markets and the sneaks;
Peaceful are the Garfinkle ping-pong balls
And peaceful are the blooms beneath the sea
Peaceful are the unreserved airplane loops and the popularly guided blips
Also the Robert Herrick stone sings a peaceful song
And the banana factory is getting hip, and the pigs' Easter party too is
   beginning to join in a general celebration
And the women and men of old Peru and young Haifa and ancient
   Japan and beautiful young rippling Lake Tahoe
And hairy old Boston and young Freeport and young Santo Domingo
   and old father Candelabra the Chieftain of Hoboes
Are rolling around the parapets for peace, and now the matadors are
   throwing in
Huge blops of canvas and the postgraduates are filling in
As grocery dates at peanut dances and the sunlight is filling in
Every human world canvas with huge and luminous pleasure gobs of
   peace—
And the Tintorettos are looking very purple for peace
And the oyster campus is beginning its peaceful song—

Oh let it be concluded, including the medals!
Peace will come thrusting out of the sky
Tomorrow morning, to bomb us into quietude.
For a while we can bid goodbye
To the frenesies of this poem, The Pleasures of Peace.
When there is peace we will not need anything but bread
Stars and plaster with which to begin.
Roaming from one beard to another we shall take the tin
From the mines and give it to roaring Fidel Castro.
Where Mao Tse Tung lies buried in ocean fields of sleeping cars

Our Lorcaesque decisions will clonk him out
And resurrect him to the rosebuddy sky
Of early evening. And the whip-shaped generals of Hanoi
Shall be taken in overcoats to visit the sky
And the earth will be gasping for joy!

"A wonder!" "A rout!" "No need now for any further poems!" "A
    Banzai for peace!" "He can speak to us all!"
And "Great, man!" "Impressive!" "Something new for you, Ken!"
    "Astounding!" "A real
Epic!" "The worst poem I have ever read!" "Abominably tasteless!"
    "Too funny!" "Dead, man!
A cop-out! a real white man's poem! a folderol of honky blank
    spitzenburger smugglerout Caucasian gyp
Of phony bourgeois peace poetry, a total shrig!" "Terrific!" "I will
    expect you at six!"
"A lovely starry catalogue for peace!" "Is it Shakespeare or Byron who
    breathes
In the lines of his poem?" "You have given us the Pleasures of Peace,
Now where is the real thing?" "Koch has studied his history!" "Bold!"
    "Stunning!" "It touches us like leaves
Sparkling in April—but is that all there is
To his peace plea?" Well, you be the one
To conclude it, if you think it needs more—I want to end it,
I want to see real Peace again! Oh peace bams!
I need your assistance—and peace drams, distilling through the world!
    peace lamps, be shining! and peace lambs, rumble up the shore!
O Goddess, sweet Muse, I'm stopping—now show us where you are!

And the big boats come sailing into the harbor for peace
And the little apes are running around the jungle for peace
And the day (that is, the star of day, the sun) is shining for peace
Somewhere a moustachioed student is puzzling over the works of
    Raymond Roussel for peace
And the Mediterranean peach trees are fast asleep for peace
With their pink arms akimbo and the blue plums of Switzerland for
    peace

And the monkeys are climbing for coconuts and peace
The Hawaiian palm
And serpents are writhing for peace—those are snakes—
And the Alps, Mount Vesuvius, all the really big important mountains
Are rising for peace, and they're filled with rocks—surely it won't be
    long;
And Leonardo da Vinci's *Last Supper* is moving across the monastery
    wall
A few micrometers for peace, and Paolo Uccello's red horses
Are turning a little redder for peace, and the Anglo-Saxon dining hall
Begins glowing like crazy, and Beowulf, Robert E. Lee, Sir Barbarossa,
    and Baron Jeep
Are sleeping on the railways for peace and darting around the harbor
And leaping into the sailboats and the sailboats will go on
And underneath the sailboats the sea will go on and we will go on
And the birds will go on and the snappy words will go on
And the tea sky and the sloped marine sky
And the hustle of beans will go on and the unserious canoe
It will all be going on in connection with you, peace, and my poem,
    like a Cadillac of wampum
Unredeemed and flying madly, will go exploding through
New cities sweet inflated, planispheres, ingenious hair, a camera smashing
Badinage, cerebral stands of atmospheres, unequaled, dreamed of
Empeacements, candled piers, fumisteries, emphatic moods, terrestrialism's
Crackle, love's flat, sun's sweets, O Peace, to you.

from

The
Art of
Love

The Circus

I remember when I wrote The Circus
I was living in Paris, or rather we were living in Paris
Janice, Frank was alive, the Whitney Museum
Was still on 8th Street, or was it still something else?
Fernand Léger lived in our building
Well it wasn't really our building it was the building we lived in
Next to a Grand Guignol troupe who made a lot of noise
So that one day I yelled through a hole in the wall
Of our apartment I don't know why there was a hole there
Shut up! And the voice came back to me saying something
I don't know what. Once I saw Léger walk out of the building
I think. Stanley Kunitz came to dinner. I wrote The Circus
In two tries, the first getting most of the first stanza;
That fall I also wrote an opera libretto called Louisa or Matilda.
Jean-Claude came to dinner. He said (about "cocktail sauce")
It should be good on something but not on these (oysters).
By that time I think I had already written The Circus.
Part of the inspiration came while walking to the post office one night
And I wrote a big segment of The Circus
When I came back, having been annoyed to have to go
I forget what I went there about
You were back in the apartment what a dump actually we liked it
I think with your hair and your writing and the pans
Moving strummingly about the kitchen and I wrote The Circus
It was a summer night no it was an autumn one summer when
I remember it but actually no autumn that black dusk toward the post
    office
And I wrote many other poems then but The Circus was the best
Maybe not by far the best there was also Geography
And the Airplane Betty poems (inspired by you) but The Circus was the
    best.

Sometimes I feel I actually am the person
Who did this, who wrote that, including that poem The Circus
But sometimes on the other hand I don't.
There are so many factors engaging our attention!

At every moment the happiness of others, the health of those we know
    and our own!
And the millions upon millions of people we don't know and their
    well-being to think about
So it seems strange I found time to write The Circus
And even spent two evenings on it, and that I have also the time
To remember that I did it, and remember you and me then, and write
    this poem about it.
At the beginning of The Circus
The Circus girls are rushing through the night
In the circus wagons and tulips and other flowers will be picked
A long time from now this poem wants to get off on its own
Someplace like a painting not held to a depiction of composing The
    Circus.

Noel Lee was in Paris then but usually out of it
In Germany or Denmark giving a concert
As part of an endless activity
Which was either his career or his happiness or a combination of both
Or neither I remember his dark eyes looking he was nervous
With me perhaps because of our days at Harvard.

It is understandable enough to be nervous with anybody!

How softly and easily one feels when alone
Love of one's friends when one is commanding the time and space
    syndrome
If that's the right word which I doubt but together how come one is so
    nervous?
One is not always but what was I then and what am I now attempting
    to create
If create is the right word
Out of this combination of experience and aloneness
And who are you telling me it is or is not a poem (not you)? Go back
    with me though
To those nights I was writing The Circus.
Do you like that poem? have you read it? It is in my book Thank You

Which Grove just reprinted. I wonder how long I am going to live
And what the rest will be like I mean the rest of my life.

John Cage said to me the other night How old are you? and I told him
    forty-six
(Since then I've become forty-seven) he said
Oh that's a great age I remember.
John Cage once told me he didn't charge much for his mushroom
    identification course (at the New School)
Because he didn't want to make a profit from nature.

He was ahead of his time I was behind my time we were both in time
Brilliant go to the head of the class and "time is a river"
It doesn't seem like a river to me it seems like an unformed plan
Days go by and still nothing is decided about
What to do until you know it never will be and then you say "time"
But you really don't care much about it any more
Time means something when you have the major part of yours ahead of
    you
As I did in Aix-en-Provence that was three years before I wrote The
    Circus
That year I wrote Bricks and The Great Atlantic Rainway
I felt time surround me like a blanket endless and soft
I could go to sleep endlessly and wake up and still be in it
But I treasured secretly the part of me that was individually changing
Like Noel Lee I was interested in my career
And still am but now it is like a town I don't want to leave
Not a tower I am climbing opposed by ferocious enemies.

I never mentioned my friends in my poems at the time I wrote The
    Circus
Although they meant almost more than anything to me
Of this now for some time I've felt an attenuation
So I'm mentioning them maybe this will bring them back to me
Not them perhaps but what I felt about them
John Ashbery Jane Freilicher Larry Rivers Frank O'Hara
Their names alone bring tears to my eyes
As seeing Polly did last night.

It is beautiful at any time but the paradox is leaving it
In order to feel it when you've come back the sun has declined
And the people are merrier or else they've gone home altogether
And you are left alone well you put up with that your sureness is like
    the sun
While you have it but when you don't its lack's a black and icy night. I
    came home

And wrote The Circus that night, Janice. I didn't come and speak to you
And put my arm around you and ask you if you'd like to take a walk
Or go to the Cirque Medrano though that's what I wrote poems about
And am writing about that now, and now I'm alone

And this is not as good a poem as The Circus
And I wonder if any good will come of either of them all the same.

The Magic of Numbers

THE MAGIC OF NUMBERS—1

How strange it was to hear the furniture being moved around in the
   apartment upstairs!
I was twenty-six, and you were twenty-two.

THE MAGIC OF NUMBERS—2

You asked me if I wanted to run, but I said no and walked on.
I was nineteen, and you were seven.

THE MAGIC OF NUMBERS—3

Yes, but does X really like us?
We were both twenty-seven.

THE MAGIC OF NUMBERS—4

You look like Jerry Lewis (1950).

THE MAGIC OF NUMBERS—5

Grandfather and grandmother want you to go over to their house for
   dinner.
They were sixty-nine, and I was two and a half.

THE MAGIC OF NUMBERS—6

One day when I was twenty-nine years old I met you and nothing
   happened.

THE MAGIC OF NUMBERS—7

No, of course it wasn't I who came to the library!
Brown eyes, flushed cheeks, brown hair. I was twenty-nine, and you
    were sixteen.

THE MAGIC OF NUMBERS—8

After we made love one night in Rockport I went outside and kissed
    the road
I felt so carried away. I was twenty-three, and you were nineteen.

THE MAGIC OF NUMBERS—9

I was twenty-nine, and so were you. We had a very passionate time.
Everything I read turned into a story about you and me, and everything
    I did was turned into a poem.

Alive for an Instant

I have a bird in my head and a pig in my stomach
And a flower in my genitals and a tiger in my genitals
And a lion in my genitals and I am after you but I have a song in my
    heart
And my song is a dove
I have a man in my hands I have a woman in my shoes
I have a landmark decision in my reason
I have a death rattle in my nose I have summer in my brain water
I have dreams in my toes
This is the matter with me and the hammer of my mother and father
Who created me with everything
But I lack calm I lack rose
Though I do not lack extreme delicacy of rose petal
Who is it that I wish to astonish?
In the birdcall I found a reminder of you
But it was thin and brittle and gone in an instant
Has nature set out to be a great entertainer?
Obviously not A great reproducer? A great Nothing?
Well I will leave that up to you
I have a knocking woodpecker in my heart and I think I have three
    souls
One for love one for poetry and one for acting out my insane self
Not insane but boring but perpendicular but untrue but true
The three rarely sing together take my hand it's active
The active ingredient in it is a touch
I am Lord Byron I am Percy Shelley I am Ariosto
I eat the bacon I went down the slide I have a thunderstorm in my
    inside I will never hate you
But how can this maelstrom be appealing? do you like menageries? my
    god
Most people want a man! So here I am
I have a pheasant in my reminders I have a goshawk in my clouds
Whatever is it which has led all these animals to you?
A resurrection? or maybe an insurrection? an inspiration?
I have a baby in my landscape and I have a wild rat in my secrets from
    you.

Some General Instructions

Do not bake bread in an oven that is not made of stone
Or you risk having imperfect bread. Byron wrote,
"The greatest pleasure in life is drinking hock
And soda water the morning after, when one has
A hangover," or words to that effect. It is a
Pleasure, for me, of the past. I do not drink so much
Any more. And when I do, I am not in sufficiently good
Shape to enjoy the hock and seltzer in the morning.
I am envious of this pleasure as I think of it. Do not
You be envious. In fact I cannot tell envy
From wish and desire and sharing imperfectly
What others have got and not got. But *envy* is a good word
To use, as *hate* is, and *lust,* because they make their point
In the worst and most direct way, so that as a
Result one is able to deal with them and go on one's way.
I read *Don Juan* twenty years ago, and six years later
I wrote a poem in emulation of it. I began
Searching for another stanza but gave in
To the ottava rima after a while, after I'd tried
Some practice stanzas in it; it worked so well
It was too late to stop, it seemed to me. Do not
Be in too much of a hurry to emulate what
You admire. Sometimes it may take a number of years
Before you are ready, but there it is, building
Inside you, a constructing egg. Low-slung
Buildings are sometimes dangerous to walk in and
Out of. A building should be at least one foot and a half
Above one's height, so that if one leaps
In surprise or joy or fear, one's head will not be injured.
Very high ceilings such as those in Gothic
Churches are excellent for giving a spiritual feeling.
Low roofs make one feel like a mole in general. But
Smallish rooms can be cozy. Many tiny people
In a little room make an amusing sight. Large
Persons, both male and female, are best seen out of doors.
Ships sided against a canal's side may be touched and
Patted, but sleeping animals should not be, for

They may bite, in anger and surprise. Of all animals
The duck is seventeenth lowliest, the eagle not as high
On the list as one would imagine, rating
Only ninety-fifth. The elephant is either two or four
Depending on the author of the list, and the tiger
Is seven. The lion is three or six. Blue is the
Favorite color of many people because the sky
Is blue and the sea is blue and many people's eyes
Are blue, but blue is not popular in those countries
Where it is the color of mold. In Spain blue
Symbolizes cowardice. In America it symbolizes "Americanness."
The racial mixture in North America should
Not be misunderstood. The English came here first,
And the Irish and the Germans and the Dutch. There were
Some French here also. The Russians, the Jews, and
The Blacks came afterwards. The women are only coming now
To a new kind of prominence in America, where Liberation
Is their byword. Giraffes, which people ordinarily
Associate with Africa, can be seen in many urban zoos
All over the world. They are an adaptable animal,
As Greek culture was an adaptable culture. Rome
Spread it all over the world. You should know,
Before it did, Alexander spread it as well. Read
As many books as you can without reading interfering
With your time for living. Boxing was formerly illegal
In England, and also, I believe, in America. If
You feel a law is unjust, you may work to change it.
It is not true, as many people say, that
That is just the way things are. Or, Those are the rules,
Immutably. The rules can be changed, although
It may be a slow process. When decorating a window, you
Should try to catch the eye of the passer-by, then
Hold it; he or she should become constantly more
Absorbed in what is being seen. Stuffed animal toys should be
Fluffy and a pleasure to hold in the hands. They
Should not be too resistant, nor should they be made
With any poisonous materials. Be careful not to set fire

To a friend's house. When covering over
A gas stove with paper or inflammable plastic
So you can paint the kitchen without injuring the stove,
Be sure there is no pilot light, or that it is out.
Do not take pills too quickly when you think you have a cold
Or other minor ailment, but wait and see if it
Goes away by itself, as many processes do
Which are really part of something else, not
What we suspected. Raphael's art is no longer as popular
As it was fifty years ago, but an aura
Still hangs about it, partly from its former renown.
The numbers seven and eleven are important to remember in dice
As are the expressions "hard eight," "Little Joe," and "fever,"
Which means *five*. Girls in short skirts when they
Kneel to play dice are beautiful, and even if they
Are not very rich or good rollers, may be
Pleasant as a part of the game. Saint Ursula
And her eleven thousand virgins has
Recently been discovered to be a printer's mistake;
There were only eleven virgins, not eleven thousand.
This makes it necessary to append a brief explanation
When speaking of Apollinaire's parody *Les
Onze Mille Verges,* which means eleven thousand
Male sexual organs—or sticks, for beating. It is a pornographic book.
Sexual information should be obtained while one is young
Enough to enjoy it. To learn of cunnilingus at fifty
Argues a wasted life. One may be tempted to
Rush out into the streets of Hong Kong or
Wherever one is and try to do too much all in one day.
Birds should never be chased out of a nature sanctuary
And shot. Do not believe the beauty of people's faces
Is a sure indication of virtue. The days of
Allegory are over. The Days of Irony are here.
Irony and Deception. But do not harden your heart. Remain
Kind and flexible. Travel a lot. By all means
Go to Greece. Meet persons of various social
Orders. Morocco should be visited by foot,

Siberia by plane. Do not be put off by
Thinking of mortality. You live long enough. There
Would, if you lived longer, never be any new
People. Enjoy the new people you see. Put your hand out
And touch that girl's arm. If you are
Able to, have children. When taking pills, be sure
You know what they are. Avoid cholesterol. In conversation
Be understanding and witty, in order that you may give
Comfort and excitement at the same time. This is the high road to
    popularity
And social success, but it is also good
For your soul and for your sense of yourself. Be supportive of others
At the expense of your wit, not otherwise. No
Joke is worth hurting someone deeply. Avoid contagious diseases.
If you do not have money, you must probably earn some
But do it in a way that is pleasant and does
Not take too much time. Painting ridiculous pictures
Is one good way, and giving lectures about yourself is another.
I once had the idea of importing tropical birds
From Africa to America, but the test cage of birds
All died on the ship, so I was unable to become
Rich that way. Another scheme I had was
To translate some songs from French into English, but
No one wanted to sing them. Living outside Florence
In February, March, and April was an excellent idea
For me, and may be for you, although I recently revisited
The place where I lived, and it is now more "built up";
Still, a little bit further out, it is not, and the fruit trees
There seem the most beautiful in the world. Every day
A new flower would appear in the garden, or every other day,
And I was able to put all this in what I wrote. I let
The weather and the landscape be narrative in me. To make money
By writing, though, was difficult. So I taught
English in a university in spite of my fear that
I knew nothing. Do not let your fear of ignorance keep you
From teaching, if that would be good for you, nor
Should you let your need for success interfere with what you love,

In fact, to do. Things have a way of working out
Which is nonsensical, and one should try to see
How that process works. If you can understand chance,
You will be lucky, for luck is what chance is about
To become, in a human context, either
Good luck or bad. You should visit places that
Have a lot of savor for you. You should be glad
To be alive. You must try to be as good as you can.
I do not know what virtue is in an absolute way,
But in the particular it is excellence which does not harm
The material but ennobles and refines it. So, honesty
Ennobles the heart and harms not the person or the coins
He remembers to give back. So, courage ennobles the heart
And the bearer's body; and tenderness refines the touch.
The problem of being good and also doing what one wishes
Is not as difficult as it seems. It is, however,
Best to get embarked early on one's dearest desires.
Be attentive to your dreams. They are usually about sex,
But they deal with other things as well in an indirect fashion
And contain information that you should have.
You should also read poetry. Do not eat too many bananas.
In the springtime, plant. In the autumn, harvest.
In the summer and winter, exercise. Do not put
Your finger inside a clam shell or
It may be snapped off by the living clam. Do not wear a shirt
More than two times without sending it to the laundry.
Be a bee fancier only if you have a face net. Avoid flies,
Hornets, and wasps. Clasp other people's hands firmly
When you are introduced to them. Say "I am glad to meet you!"
Be able to make a mouth and cheeks like a fish. It
Is entertaining. Speaking in accents
Can also entertain people. But do not think
Mainly of being entertaining. Think of your death.
Think of the death of the fish you just imitated. Be artistic, and be
  unfamiliar.
Think of the blue sky, how artists have
Imitated it. Think of your secretest thoughts,

How poets have imitated them. Think of what you feel
Secretly, and how music has imitated that. Make a moue.
Get faucets for every water outlet in your
House. You may like to spend some summers on
An island. Buy woolen material in Scotland and have
The cloth cut in London, lapels made in France.
Become religious when you are tired of everything
Else. As a little old man or woman, die
In a fine and original spirit that is yours alone.
When you are dead, waste, and make room for the future.
Do not make tea from water which is already boiling.
Use the water just as it starts to boil. Otherwise
It will not successfully "draw" the tea, or
The tea will not successfully "draw" it. Byron
Wrote that no man under thirty should ever see
An ugly woman, suggesting desire should be so strong
It affected the princeliest of senses; and Schopenhauer
Suggested the elimination of the human species
As the way to escape from the Will, which he saw as a monstrous
Demon-like force which destroys us. When
Pleasure is mild, you should enjoy it, and
When it is violent, permit it, as far as
You can, to enjoy you. Pain should be
Dealt with as efficiently as possible. To "cure" a dead octopus
You hold it by one leg and bang it against a rock.
This makes a noise heard all around the harbor,
But it is necessary, for otherwise the meat would be too tough.
Fowl are best plucked by humans, but machines
Are more humanitarian, since extended chicken
Plucking is an unpleasant job. Do not eat unwashed beets
Or rare pork, nor should you gobble uncooked dough.
Fruits, vegetables, and cheese make an excellent diet.
You should understand some science. Electricity
Is fascinating. Do not be defeated by the
Feeling that there is too much for you to know. That
Is a myth of the oppressor. You are
Capable of understanding life. And it is yours alone

And only this time. Someone who excites you
Should be told so, and loved, if you can, but no one
Should be able to shake you so much that you wish to
Give up. The sensations you feel are caused by outside
Phenomena and inside impulses. Whatever you
Experience is both "a person out there" and a dream
As well as unwashed electrons. It is your task to see this through
To a conclusion that makes sense to all concerned.
Now go. You cannot come back until these lessons are learned
And you can show that you have learned them for yourself.

The Art of Poetry

To write a poem, perfect physical condition
Is desirable but not necessary. Keats wrote
In poor health, as did D. H. Lawrence. A combination
Of disease and old age is an impediment to writing, but
Neither is, alone, unless there is arteriosclerosis—that is,
Hardening of the arteries—but that we shall count as a disease
Accompanying old age and therefore a negative condition.
Mental health is certainly not a necessity for the
Creation of poetic beauty, but a degree of it
Would seem to be, except in rare cases. Schizophrenic poetry
Tends to be loose, disjointed, uncritical of itself, in some ways
Like what is best in our modern practice of the poetic art
But unlike it in others, in its lack of concern
For intensity and nuance. A few great poems
By poets supposed to be "mad" are of course known to us all,
Such as those of Christopher Smart, but I wonder how crazy they were,
These poets who wrote such contraptions of exigent art?
As for Blake's being "crazy," that seems to me very unlikely.

But what about Wordsworth? Not crazy, I mean, but what about his
    later work, boring
To the point of inanity, almost, and the destructive "corrections" he
    made
To his *Prelude,* as it nosed along, through the shallows of art?
He was really terrible after he wrote the "Ode:
Intimations of Immortality from Recollections of Early Childhood," for
    the most part,
Or so it seems to me. Walt Whitman's "corrections," too, of the *Leaves
    of Grass,*
And especially "Song of Myself," are almost always terrible.

Is there some way to ride to old age and to fame and acceptance
And pride in oneself and the knowledge society approves one
Without getting lousier and lousier and depleted of talent? Yes,
Yeats shows it could be. And Sophocles wrote poetry until he was a
    hundred and one,
Or a hundred, anyway, and drank wine and danced all night.

113

But he was an Ancient Greek and so may not help us here. On
The other hand, he may. There is, it would seem, a sense
In which one must grow and develop, and yet stay young—
Not peroxide, not stupid, not transplanting hair to look peppy,
But young in one's heart. And for this it is a good idea to have some
Friends who write as well as you do, who know what you are doing,
And know when you are doing something wrong.
They should have qualities that you can never have,
To keep you continually striving up an impossible hill.
These friends should supply such competition as will make you, at times,
    very uncomfortable.
And you should take care of your physical body as well
As of your poetic heart, since consecutive hours of advanced
    concentration
Will be precious to your writing and may not be possible
If you are exhausted and ill. Sometimes an abnormal or sick state
Will be inspiring, and one can allow oneself a certain number,
But they should not be the rule. Drinking alcohol is all right
If not in excess, and I would doubt that it would be beneficial
During composition itself. As for marijuana, there are those who
Claim to be able to write well under its influence
But I have yet to see the first evidence for such claims.
Stronger drugs are ludicrously inappropriate, since they destroy judgment
And taste, and make one either like or dislike everything one does,
Or else turn life into a dream. One does not write well in one's sleep.

As for following fashionable literary movements,
It is almost irresistible, and for a while I can see no harm in it,
But the sooner you find your own style the better off you will be.
Then all "movements" fit into it. You have an "exercycle" of your own.
Trying out all kinds of styles and imitating poets you like
And incorporating anything valuable you may find there,
These are sound procedures, and in fact I think even essential
To the perfection of an original style which is yours alone.
An original style may not last more than four years,
Or even three or even two, sometimes on rare occasions one,
And then you must find another. It is conceivable even that a style
For a very exigent poet would be for one work only,

After which it would be exhausted, limping, unable to sustain any
   wrong or right.
By "exigent" I mean extremely careful, wanting each poem to be a
   conclusion
Of everything he senses, feels, and knows.
The exigent poet has his satisfactions, which are relatively special
But that is not the only kind of poet you can be. There is a pleasure in
   being Venus,
In sending love to everyone, in being Zeus,
In sending thunder to everyone, in being Apollo
And every day sending out light. It is a pleasure to write continually
And well, and that is a special poetic dream
Which you may have or you may not. Not all writers have it.
Browning once wrote a poem every day of one year
And found it "didn't work out well." But who knows?
He went on for a year—something must have been working out.
And why only one poem a day? Why not several? Why not one every
   hour for eight to ten hours a day?
There seems no reason not to try it if you have the inclination.

Some poets like "saving up" for poems, others like to spend incessantly
   what they have.
In spending, of course, you get more, there is a "bottomless pocket"
Principle involved, since your feelings are changing every instant
And the language has millions of words, and the number of
   combinations is infinite.
True, one may feel, perhaps Puritanically, that
One person can only have so much to say, and, besides, ten thousand
   poems per annum
Per person would flood the earth and perhaps eventually the universe,
And one would not want so many poems—so there is a "quota system"
Secretly, or not so secretly, at work. "If I can write one good poem a
   year,
I am grateful," the noted Poet says, or "six" or "three." Well, maybe for
   that Poet,
But for you, fellow paddler, and for me, perhaps not. Besides, I think
   poems
Are esthetecologically harmless and psychodegradable

And never would they choke the spirits of the world. For a poem only
    affects us
And "exists," really, if it is worth it, and there can't be too many of
    those.
Writing constantly, in any case, is the poetic dream
Diametrically opposed to the "ultimate distillation"
Dream, which is that of the exigent poet. Just how good a poem should
    be
Before one releases it, either from one's own work or then into the
    purview of others,
May be decided by applying the following rules: ask 1) Is it astonishing?
Am I pleased each time I read it? Does it say something I was unaware
    of
Before I sat down to write it? and 2) Do I stand up from it a better
    man
Or a wiser, or both? or can the two not be separated? 3) Is it really by
    me
Or have I stolen it from somewhere else? (This sometimes happens,
Though it is comparatively rare.) 4) Does it reveal something about me
I never want anyone to know? 5) Is it sufficiently "modern"?
(More about this a little later) 6) Is it in my own "voice"?
Along with, of course, the more obvious questions, such as
7) Is there any unwanted awkwardness, cheap effects, asking
    illegitimately for attention,
Show-offiness, cuteness, pseudo-profundity, old hat checks,
Unassimilated dream fragments, or other "literary,"
    "kiss-me-I'm-poetical" junk?
Is my poem free of this? 8) Does it move smoothly and swiftly
From excitement to dream and then come flooding reason
With purity and soundness and joy? 9) Is this the kind of poem
I would envy in another if he could write? 10)
Would I be happy to go to Heaven with this pinned on to my
Angelic jacket as an entrance show? Oh, would I? And if you can
    answer to all these Yes
Except for the 4th one, to which the answer should be No,
Then you can release it, at least for the time being.

I would look at it again, though, perhaps in two hours, then after one
  or two weeks,
And then a month later, at which time you can probably be sure.

To look at a poem again of course causes anxiety
In many cases, but that pain a writer must learn to endure,
For without it he will be like a chicken which never knows what it is
  doing
And goes feathering and fluttering through life. When one finds the
  poem
Inadequate, then one must revise, and this can be very hard going
Indeed. For the original "inspiration" is not there. Some poets never
  master the
Art of doing this, and remain "minor" or almost nothing at all.
Such have my sympathy but not my praise. My sympathy because
Such work is difficult, and most persons accomplish nothing whatsoever
In the course of their lives; at least these poets are writing
"First versions," but they can never win the praise
Of a discerning reader until they take hard-hearted Revision to bed
And bend her to their will and create through her "second-time-around"
  poems
Or even "third-time-around" ones. There are several ways to win
The favors of this lady. One is unstinting labor, but be careful
You do not ruin what is already there by unfeeling rewriting
That makes it more "logical" but cuts out its heart.
Sometimes neglecting a poem for several weeks is best,
As if you had forgotten you wrote it, and changing it then
As swiftly as you can—in that way, you will avoid at least dry
  "re-detailing"
Which is fatal to any art. Sometimes the confidence you have from a
  successful poem
Can help you to find for another one the changes you want.
Actually, a night's sleep and a new day filled with confidence are very
  desirable,
And, once you get used to the ordinary pains that go with revising,
You may grow to like it very much. It gives one the strange feeling
That one is "working on" something, as an engineer does, or a pilot

When something goes wrong with the plane; whereas the inspired first
	version of a poem
Is more like simply a lightning flash to the heart.
Revising gives one the feeling of being a builder. And if it brings pain?
	Well,
It sometimes does, and women have pain giving birth to children
Yet often wish to do so again, and perhaps the grizzly bear has pain
Burrowing down into the ground to sleep all winter. In writing
The pain is relatively minor. We need not speak of it again
Except in the case of the fear that one has "lost one's talent,"
Which I will go into immediately. This fear
Is a perfectly logical fear for poets to have,
And all of them, from time to time, have it. It is very rare
For what one does best and that on which one's happiness depends
To so large an extent, to be itself dependent on factors
Seemingly beyond one's control. For whence cometh Inspiration?
Will she stay in her Bower of Bliss or come to me this evening?
Have I gotten too old for her kisses? Will she like that boy there rather
	than me?
Am I a dried-up old hog? Is this then the end of it? Haven't I
Lost that sweet easy knack I had last week,
Last month, last year, last decade, which pleased everyone
And especially pleased me? I no longer can feel the warmth of it—
Oh, I have indeed lost it! Etcetera. And when you write a new poem
You like, you forget this anguish, and so on till your death,
Which you'll be remembered beyond, not for "keeping your talent,"
But for what you wrote, in spite of your worries and fears.

The truth is, I think, that one does not lose one's talent,
Although one can misplace it—in attempts to remain in the past,
In profitless ventures intended to please those whom
Could one see them clearly one would not wish to please,
In opera librettos, or even in one's life
Somewhere. But you can almost always find it, perhaps in trying new
	forms
Or not in form at all but in the (seeming) lack of it—
Write "stream of consciousness." Or, differently again, do some
	translations.

Renounce repeating the successes of the years before. Seek
A success of a type undreamed of. Write a poetic fishing manual. Try an
    Art of Love.
Whatever, be on the lookout for what you feared you had lost,
The talent you misplaced. The only ways really to lose it
Are serious damage to the brain or being so attracted
To something else (such as money, sex, repairing expensive engines)
That you forget it completely. In that case, how care that it is lost?
In spite of the truth of all this, however, I am aware
That fear of lost talent is a natural part of a poet's existence.
So be prepared for it, and do not let it get you down.

Just how much experience a poet should have
To be sure he has enough to be sure he is an adequate knower
And feeler and thinker of experience as it exists in our time
Is a tough one to answer, and the only sure rule I can think of
Is experience as much as you can and write as much as you can.
These two can be contradictory. A great many experiences are worthless
At least as far as poetry is concerned. Whereas the least promising,
Seemingly, will throw a whole epic in one's lap. However, that is
    Sarajevo
And not cause. Probably. I do not know what to tell you
That would apply to all cases. I would suggest travel
And learning at least one other language (five or six
Could be a distraction). As for sexuality and other
Sensual pleasures, you must work that out for yourself.
You should know the world, men, women, space, wind, islands,
    governments,
The history of art, news of the lost continents, plants, evenings,
Mornings, days. But you must also have time to write.
You need environments for your poems and also people,
But you also need life, you need to care about these things
And these persons, and that is the difficulty, that
What you will find best to write about cannot be experienced
Merely as "material." There are some arts one picks up
Of "living sideways," and forwards and backwards at the same time,
But they often do not work—or do, to one's disadvantage:
You feel, "I did not experience that. That cow did

More than I. Or that 'Blue Man' without a thought in the world
Beyond existing. He is the one who really exists.
That is true poetry. I am nothing." I suggest waiting a few hours
Before coming to such a rash decision and going off
Riding on a camel yourself. For you cannot escape your mind
And your strange interest in writing poetry, which will make you,
Necessarily, an experiencer and un-experiencer
Of life at the same time, but you should realize that what you do
Is immensely valuable, and difficult, too, in a way riding a camel is not,
Though that is valuable too—you two will amaze each other,
The Blue Man and you, and that is also a part of life
Which you must catch in your poem. As for how much one's poetry
Should "reflect one's experience," I do not think it can avoid
Doing that. The naïve version of such a concern
Of course is stupid, but if you feel the need to "confront"
Something, try it, and see how it goes. To "really find your emotions,"
Write, and keep working at it. Success in the literary world
Is mostly irrelevant but may please you. It is good to have a friend
To help you past the monsters on the way. Becoming famous will not
    hurt you
Unless you are foolishly overcaptivated and forget
That this too is merely a part of your "experience." For those who make
    poets famous
In general know nothing about poetry. Remember your obligation is to
    write,
And, in writing, to be serious without being solemn, fresh without being
    cold,
To be inclusive without being asinine, particular
Without being picky, feminine without being effeminate,
Masculine without being brutish, human while keeping all the animal
    graces
You had inside the womb, and beast-like without being inhuman.
Let your language be delectable always, and fresh and true.
Don't be conceited. Let your compassion guide you
And your excitement. And always bring your endeavors to their end.

One thing a poem needs is to be complete
In itself and not need others to complement it.

Therefore this poem about writing should be complete
With information about everything concerned in the act
Of creating a poem. A work also should not be too long.
Each line should give a gathered new sensation
Of "Oh, now I know that, and want to go on!"
"Measure," which decides how long a poem should be,
Is difficult, because possible elaboration is endless,
As endless as the desire to write, so the decision to end
A poem is generally arbitrary yet must be made
Except in the following two cases: when one embarks on an epic
Confident that it will last all one's life,
Or when one deliberately continues it past hope of concluding—
Edmund Spenser and Ezra Pound seem examples
Of one of these cases or the other. And no one knows how
The Faerie Queene continued (if it did, as one writer said,
The last parts destroyed in the sacking of Spenser's house
By the crazed but justified Irish, or was it by his servants?).
It may be that Spenser never went beyond Book Six
In any serious way, because the thought of ending was unpleasant,
Yet his plan for the book, if he wrote on, would oblige him to end it.
    This unlike Pound
Who had no set determined place to cease. Coming to a stop
And giving determined form is easiest in drama,
It may be, or in short songs, like "We'll Go
No More a-Roving," one of Byron's most
Touching poems, an absolute success, the best
Short one, I believe, that Byron wrote. In all these
Cases, then, except for "lifetime" poems, there is a point one reaches
When one knows that one must come to an end,
And that is the point that must be reached. To reach it, however,
One may have to cut out much of what one has written along the way,
For the end does not necessarily come of itself
But must be coaxed forth from the material, like a blossom.

Anyone who would like to write an epic poem
May wish to have a plot in mind, or at least a mood—the
Minimum requirement is a form. Sometimes a stanza,
Like Spenser's, or Ariosto's ottava rima, will set the poem going

Downhill and uphill and all around experience
And the world in the maddest way imaginable. Enough,
In this case, to begin, and to let oneself be carried
By the wind of eight (or, in the case of Spenser, nine) loud rhymes.
Sometimes blank verse will tempt the amateur
Of endless writing; sometimes a couplet; sometimes "free verse."
"Skeltonics" are hard to sustain over an extended period
As are, in English, and in Greek for all I know, "Sapphics."
The epic has a clear advantage over any sort of lyric
Poem in being there when you go back to it to continue. The
Lyric is fleeting, usually caught in one
Breath or not at all (though see what has been said before
About revision—it can be done). The epic one is writing, however,
Like a great sheep dog is always there
Wagging and waiting to welcome one into the corner
To be petted and sent forth to fetch a narrative bone.
O writing an epic! what a pleasure you are
And what an agony! But the pleasure is greater than the agony,
And the achievement is the sweetest thing of all. Men raise the problem,
"How can one write an epic in the modern world?" One can answer,
"Look around you—tell me how one cannot!" Which is more or less
    what
Juvenal said about Satire, but epic is a form
Our international time-space plan cries out for—or so it seems
To one observer. The lyric is a necessity too,
And those you may write either alone
Or in the interstices of your epic poem, like flowers
Crannied in the Great Wall of China as it sweeps across the earth.
To write only lyrics is to be sad, perhaps,
Or fidgety, or overexcited, too dependent on circumstance—
But there is a way out of that. The lyric must be bent
Into a more operative form, so that
Fragments of being reflect absolutes (see for example the verse of
William Carlos Williams or Frank O'Hara), and you can go on
Without saying it all every time. If you can master the knack of it,
You are a fortunate poet, and a skilled one. You should read
A great deal, and be thinking of writing poetry all the time.

Total absorption in poetry is one of the finest things in existence—
It should not make you feel guilty. Everyone is absorbed in something.
The sailor is absorbed in the sea. Poetry is the mediation of life.

The epic is particularly appropriate to our contemporary world
Because we are so uncertain of everything and also know too much,
A curious and seemingly contradictory condition, which the epic salves
By giving us our knowledge and our grasp, with all our lack of control
    as well.
The lyric adjusts to us like a butterfly, then epically eludes our grasp.
Poetic drama in our time seems impossible but actually exists as
A fabulous possibility just within our reach. To write drama
One must conceive of an answerer to what one says, as I am now
    conceiving of you.

As to whether or not you use rhyme and how "modern" you are
It is something your genius can decide on every morning
When you get out of bed. What a clear day! Good luck at it!
Though meter is probably, and rhyme too, probably, dead
For a while, except in narrative stanzas. You try it out.
The pleasure of the easy inflection between meter and these easy vocable
    lines
Is a pleasure, if you are able to have it, you are unlikely to renounce.
As for "surrealistic" methods and techniques, they have become a
Natural part of writing. Your poetry, if possible, should be extended
Somewhat beyond your experience, while still remaining true to it;
Unconscious material should play a luscious part
In what you write, since without the unconscious part
You know very little; and your plainest statements should be
Even better than plain. A reader should put your work down puzzled,
Distressed, and illuminated, ready to believe
It is curious to be alive. As for your sense of what good you
Do by writing, compared to what good statesmen, doctors,
Flower salesmen, and missionaries do, perhaps you do less
And perhaps more. If you would like to try one of these
Other occupations for a while, try it. I imagine you will find
That poetry does something they do not do, whether it is

More important or not, and if you like poetry, you will like doing that
    yourself.

Poetry need not be an exclusive occupation.
Some think it should, some think it should not. But you should
Have years for poetry, or at least if not years months
At certain points in your life. Weeks, days, and hours may not suffice.
Almost any amount of time suffices to be a "minor poet"
Once you have mastered a certain amount of the craft
For writing a poem, but I do not see the good of minor poetry,
Like going to the Tour d'Argent to get dinner for your dog,
Or "almost" being friends with someone, or hanging around but not
    attending a school,
Or being a nurse's aide for the rest of your life after getting a degree in
    medicine,
What is the point of it? And some may wish to write songs
And use their talent that way. Others may even end up writing ads.
To those of you who are left, when these others have departed,
And you are a strange bunch, I alone address these words.

It is true that good poetry is difficult to write.
Poetry is an escape from anxiety and a source of it as well.
On the whole, it seems to me worthwhile. At the end of a poem
One may be tempted to grow too universal, philosophical, and vague
Or to bring in History, or the Sea, but one should not do that
If one can possibly help it, since it makes
Each thing one writes sound like everything else,
And poetry and life are not like that. Now I have said enough.

On Beauty

Beauty is sometimes personified
As a beautiful woman, and this personification is satisfying
In that, probably, of all the beautiful things one sees
A beautiful person is the most inspiring, because, in looking at her,
One is swept by desires, as the sails are swept in the bay, and when the
    body is excited
Beauty is more evident, whether one is awake or asleep.
A beautiful person also suggests a way
To be at one with beauty, to be united with it, physically, with more
    than our eyes,
And strange it is, this tactile experience
Of beauty, and the subject of many other works. The first beauty one
    sees
That one is conscious of as "beauty," what is that? Some say
"The mother's face"—but I do not think
The baby is conscious of anything as "beauty"—perhaps years after
When he looks at Carpaccio's Saint Ursula, he thinks of "mother"
Subconsciously, and that is why he finds her *"bella—*
Poi anche bellissima," as he says in Italian
To the guard or fellow-viewer at his side. The guard smokes a cigarette
Later, on the steps of the palazzo, and he gazes at the blue sky,
And for him that is bellissima. Perhaps the sky reminds him
Of someone's eyes. But why is that, this human reminder,
If that is what accounts for beauty, so enchanting? Like a thigh, the
    island of Kos
Is extremely lovely, as are many other Greek islands—Lemnos,
Poros, and Charybdis. We could sail among them, happy, fortunate
To be in such places, yet tormented by an inner sense
Of anxiety and guilt, beleaguered by a feeling we had torn
Ourselves from what is really important, simply for this
Devious experiencing of "beauty," which may be nothing but a clumsy
    substitute
For seeing our mothers again. But it is not that,
Not a substitute, but something else. There is no going backwards in
Pleasure, as Hemingway wrote, in *Death in the Afternoon,* speaking of
    Manolete
Who changed the art of bullfighting around, and there is

No going backwards, either, in beauty. Mother may still be there,
In dimity or in nakedness even, but once you have seen Lemnos
It is all over for mother, and Samos and Chios and Kos, and
Once you have seen the girls of your own time. Perhaps one's earliest
  experience
Of beauty is a sort of concentrate, with which one begins,
And adds the water of a life of one's own; then
Flavors come, and colors, and flowers (if one's
Mother is Japanese, perhaps), mountains covered with flowers, and clouds
  which are the
Colors of blossoming trees. One cannot go back to a
Nightingale in the hope of getting a "more fundamental
Experience" of it than one has gotten from Keats's poem. This
Schema is not impoverishing but enriching. One does
Not have the Ode instead of the bird, one has them both. And so
With mother (although mother dies), and so with the people
We love, and with the other things of this world. What, in
Fact, is probably the case is that the thigh
And nose and forehead of a person have an interchangeable
Relationship with landscape; we see
The person first: as babies we aren't tourists, and our new-flung eyes
Are not accustomed to looking at mountains, although
Soon we see breasts—and later see the Catskills, the
Berkshires and the Alps. And as we were moved by breasts before
We are moved by mountains now. Does that mean the
World is for us to eat? that our lives are a constant re-
Gression? Or "Plato inside out"? Or might it not mean, as
I have suggested, that we are born to love either or both?

Beautiful, Charybdis, are your arms, and beautiful your hands;
Beautiful in the clear blue water are the swift white-tinted waves;
Beautiful is the "starlight" (is there any light there,
Really? We may come to the question in a while of whether
Beauty is a reflection); beautiful is the copy
Of Michelangelo's David, and the original; beautiful the regatta
Of happy days one receives, and beautiful the haymow
From which the birds have just flown away. If they

Have left some eggs there, let us go and look at them
To see if they are beautiful as well.

If all these things are carry-overs from mother,
Then mother is everywhere, she completes our consciousness
On every side and of every sight we see. We thank you, mother,
If that is so, and we will leave you there at the beginning of it all, with
    dad.

It is always a possibility that beauty does not exist
In the realest sense, but that is just as true of everything else,
So in a way it does not modify this poem but actually strengthens it
By being a part of the awareness that puts it together.

Beauty suggests endlessness and timelessness, but beauty
Is fleeting in individual instances, though a person's
Or a landscape's beauty may last for quite a long while.
It is worth preserving, by exercise, good diet, and other
Ways of keeping in good health, and in the case of
Landscape, careful gardening, and good, enforceable zoning and
Anti-pollution laws. Even though it may cause desperation
In the abstract, the thought that "beauty is only for a day,"
So to speak, in individual instances it need not. A good
Night's sleep and wake up happy at all that is beautiful now
Is the best remedy. It is just a quality of beauty that
It comes and it goes. We are contented with the ocean's
Being that way, and summer, winter, fall, and
Spring also leave and return. If beauty does not return
In all cases to the same objects, we must simply be alert and
Find it where it has gone. Every good artist knows
This, and every person should know it as well, it being
One thing one can learn from art, and of course as I said
From close study of nature—though art is sometimes easier
To learn from, whether one is viewing it or creating it.
People, of course, are often depressed,
Despite philosophy and art, about the loss of their own
Beauty, and it is a fact that once one has something

To no longer have it is a sorrow, and there is nothing
This poem can do about that. On the other hand,
You participated in it for a while (for twenty or for
Forty years) and that is pretty good. And there it is,
Shining in the world. Your own exterior is, after
All, just a tiny part of that.

Beauty quite naturally seems as if it would be beautiful
No matter how we looked at it, but this is not always true. Take a
    microscope to
Many varieties of beauty and they are gone. A young girl's
Lovely complexion, for example, reveals gigantic pores, hideously,
    gapingly
Embedded in her, as Gulliver among the Brobdingnagians observed. And
Put some of her golden hair under the microscope: huge,
Portentous, menacing tubes. But since
Our eyes aren't microscopic, who cares? To have an
Operation to make them so would be insane. A certain
Sanity is necessary for life, and even our deepest studies need not
Carry us beyond a certain place, i.e. right here, the place
Where we would get microscopic eyes. Nor is it necessary to
Pluck out the eyes of an animal (a dog, say) and
Transplant them for our own, so we can see
Beauty as a dog sees it, or as a kangaroo or as a rhinoceros.
We do not know if animals see beauty at all, or if
They merely see convenience and sex, a certain useful log here or there a
Loyalty-retaining moving creature. I do not think we need to know,
Physically, in our own bodies. To give up our human eyes,
And indeed our human brain, for those of a horse or lion might
Be fantastic to write a book about, but then we would
Never know anything else. I suggest, instead,
Walking around beautiful objects, if one can, for that
Is sometimes very pleasant and reveals newer and, if
That is possible, even more beautiful views. One's first view
Of the Bay of Baia, for example, may be improved
Sharply by the view from a boat coming into the harbor or
From the Hotel Shamrock on the mountain's peak. First sight of a girl

Is often one of best ones, but later, sighing above her in bed,
She is even more beautiful. And then in a.m. waking you up
With a happy alarm. Who would want microscopic eyes at
Such a moment? or macroscopic ones, for that matter, which would
    make
Your girl look extremely tiny, almost invisible, like an insect
You might swat, if you weren't careful; and you would feel
Funny, wondering how someone so small
Could make you feel so happy; and it would be so hallucinatory, to
Go to bed with her and hold her in your arms, for unless you had
Macrotactile arm and hand nerves as well, she would
Feel as large as you are, almost, and yet be so small! You
Would think you were stoned on something monstrous. I think
The proportion between eye and nature, then, is, as
Far as beauty goes, the most important proportion of all.

Like your own eyes, it is probably best to accept your own culture
In responding to what is beautiful. To try to transform yourself
To an Ancient Mesopotamian or a Navajo priest
In order to decide on the beauty of a stallion or a
Stone jar could end up being an impediment to actually seeing anything.
    Some
Knowledge is helpful, but you should exercise reason and control.

In general, any sort of artificial aids
To looking at something may be an impediment to beauty
Unless you are so thoroughly accustomed to them that
You do not know they are there. So a telescope,
When looking at the Valley of the Arno for the first time, may not
Give the pleasure you might get from your naked eye,
Even if your eye did not enable you to see things in
So much detail. Eyeglasses can be annoying at first, as
Well, and even such a slight thing as a map, looked at
Too closely, can keep you from enjoying the landscape it explicates.

Naturalness, important in the looking at beauty, is also esteemed
A main characteristic of the beauty of what is seen.

"Naturalness" is difficult to define, though one knows what it is
When one sees it. Greek statues, for example,
Are both more beautiful and more natural-seeming
Than the people in the harbor of Lemnos, or more natural in
A certain way. One says of a certain statue
"How natural it is!" but does not praise Astrovapoulos the butcher
Or Axanthe the waitress in the same way. It may be
It is because it would seem foolish to praise a living
Human creature for being "natural," but we do praise some—usually
    children,
Or famous or prestigious people one would not expect
To behave like everyone else, or great beauties who do not
"Put on airs"—those we'd expect to be stiff, but
Who are not, except in the case of children, but
Them we seem to be comparing to our stiffer selves. Statues,
Which are expected to be rigid, may have a strange appearance of
    motion
And ease. And in dancers one admires the same contrast
Between rigidity and movement. Where does this leave us
As we look at the ocean, then? It too is both frozen and mobile.
    Without the tides
It would probably be a great mess. And in a girl
Naturalness is real breasts and a warm, attempting smile,
Combined with bone structure and a good complexion. Pimples,
    however
Natural they may be, are rarely praised as such. Nor are
Snoring people or the deaf, though both conditions are
Natural. At the opposite, or not quite the opposite, pole from naturalness
Is strangeness, though strange need not be unnatural. Beauty seems a
    combination
Of natural and strange, which is one thing that makes it so complex
To talk about to some people, who want it to be one
Or the other: avant-garde people wishing for it always to
Be strange, "traditionalists" wanting it always to be
Natural—neither really understanding what those words mean
Or how they are related to things, since
The world is naturally strange, i.e. what seems to us natural

Is really bizarre—the composition of a human face, for
Example, or the splendors of the sun. Though strange as
Well as natural, dependent on our culture and on our vision,
Beauty is a good companion, trustworthy and cheerful.
People are right to look for a beautiful mate and to
Put windows where the beauty is outside.

Animals, though natural and strange, I do not usually find beautiful,
Or fish or insects either. I do not know why this is. Many
People feel otherwise. Birds make me think uncomfortably of color
(Except when they whiz past by surprise) and the idea of feathers
I find disturbing. Whatever its cause, a strong feeling of discomfort
Makes hard the perception of beauty. You should not worry
If some people find some things beautiful that you do not
Find so. There is probably something that seems ugly to others
Which gives you the pleasure that beauty brings
Into our lives. Such strong feelings as physical
Discomfort, or deprivation, or a terror of disease or
Death, can make beauty unlikely to get through to you. It may be
That seeing birds in a more natural, everyday way would
Make them seem more beautiful to me. I do not know
Since this has not happened. Birds are something I was told
Were "beautiful" when I was a child. Flowers also were, and
Especially roses. I am still slightly uncomfortable with
Roses. The moon and the stars were also on my parents' and
Teachers' list of what was beautiful. It has been
Hard for me to love them (stars and moon, I mean) but I have,
Despite this early "training," which may be injurious to beauty
In some cases, in others not. In raising your child,
You should share your feeling with him of what is beautiful,
But do not expect a child to respond to it that way.
He or she is likely to respond more like a poet or an artist,
By wanting to "do" something with it—to run
Through it, or eat it or tear it apart. It is in later life perhaps
Precisely the suppression of these feelings, or some of these feelings,
That results in our feeling of beauty, which we are merely to
    contemplate.

Contemplation seemed to Aristotle the superior mode, to others may
    seem an unnatural mode
Of life. Most people still feel in the presence of beauty that old wish
To do something, whether it is to make love
To the beautiful person, in the case it is a person, or if
It is a landscape or a seemingly billion stars, or a
Light blue scarcely rippling bay, to run through it, get out a
Telescope, or dive in and swim or build a boat or buy a piece of
Property adjoining it. Sometimes it is merely an impulse to
Jump up and down, or to scream, or to call people up on the telephone
    to
Tell them about what one has seen. In any case, nothing satisfies
The impulse but merely exhausts it. The perception of beauty wears out
After a while, speeded up by activity, and then one is all right again or
Not all right again, depending on how you look at it. Remembered
    beauty,
On the other hand, if protected properly, can be a source of light and
Heat to one's imagination and one's sense of life, like
The sun shining in on one's shoulder. It is difficult to make
The impression of beauty last as it is difficult to make the pleasure of
    love-
Making last for days, but it can sometimes happen. The length of time
    one stays with
Something one thinks is beautiful can help it to stay
With one, so going back through the gallery is often a good idea.
In these cases, contemplation itself is a form of activity
The object of beauty incites. But children, told to contemplate
In this way, are likely to dislike what they see
Because they cannot contemplate and thus can do nothing
With it. Beauty, along with seeming strange, natural, and being temporal
And adapted to the size of human eyes and being a concentrate
With time added, must also seem like something of one's own.
Roses and birds belonged to my mother and her friends. I loved
Tulips, daisies, daffodils, and the white
Tiny flowers whose name I don't know which grew in
The woods in back of my house, which was used as a dump (the
Woods, I mean) and which were so small they were useless for the
    decoration of homes.

One reaction beauty sometimes causes, in the absence
Of other responses, is that it makes one cry, perhaps
Because of seeming a possibility of happiness projected
Into the past, as it is, in fact, in space, which one
Can never again reach, because irrevocably behind one. It may be
That there was never any chance of the kind of happiness
Beauty suggests, and thus that our tears are
In vain, but it is hard to imagine what "useful" tears would be
After one is an adult. Crying is crying, and
Blossoming plum and cherry trees may make one cry
A good deal, as may rocky coastlines and Renaissance art.
The tears in such cases are probably caused by the conflict
Beauty sends up of "Too much! There is no way to
Deal with me!" And the presence of beauty may make
Tears easier and seem safer, too, since it seems, also, to warrant and
    protect.

If none of the actions we take in regard to beauty
Seems completely satisfactory, and if we go on feeling
An impulse to do, to finally do something when we are in its presence,
    then
It may be either that beauty is a front for something else or that
It has a purpose our minds have not penetrated yet—or both. Many
    people
Say that it is all a trick of "Nature." "Nature" makes people
Beautiful, so people will make love to each other and the
Human race will go on, which "Nature" apparently desires.
Others, and sometimes some of these same ones, assume there is
A God, a Divine Being, with absolute power, who also wishes
The human race to go on, as well as to remind them
By the beauty of mountains, lakes, and trees (as well as of human
    features)
Of how bountiful He is, so that they will do His Will. The
Human features are lovely, also, to remind them
Of what God Himself looks like (approximately). I believe
All this is too simple to be correct, but you are free to believe what you
    will.
Nor can I subscribe to the "Analogy Theory" of beauty,

That beautiful things exist to show us how to behave
To ourselves and to each other. For one thing, the correspondence
Is insufficiently clear—just how that blue sky, for example, can
Help me to do what is right. It is true that clarity and harmony
May be the result of an ethical action, but it is also
True, often, that such actions involve pain and deprivation
Which seem inimical to beauty, and which I cannot see up there at all.

The beauty of many things does seem to show
They are good for us (or good for our descendants), but
What about poison flowers and berries? Treacherous bays? Beautiful
Wolf women who simply wish to devour us? What about Blake's
    Tyger?
My own view is that we are in a situation
That is not under our control (or anyone's, for that matter) but
Which we can handle, if we are wise about it, fairly well.
Temper your admiration for beauty with whatever
Else you know of the particular example you are looking at. Do not
Leap into a reflection in a lake, or take up with a bad woman
Because her breasts are beautiful, or commit
Suicide because Botticelli's *Venus* (it is not a real
Situation) reminds you of what your life has not been. These are times
    to let the
"Enchantment" wear off for a while—for it is an
Enchantment, and it will go away. You will feel driven
To act on your feeling immediately, and—
Perhaps you should go ahead and do it, even though you will be
    destroyed.
Not every man can die for beauty. Perhaps there is some kind of List
On which your name will be recorded. I don't know. I don't know if I
    approve of that.
However, my approval may not be that which you are after.
As a young man myself I felt I would do anything for
Beauty, but actually I was fairly cautious and did
Nothing that seemed likely to result in the destruction of my ability
To stay around and have these ideas and put them into words.
I would go forward one step, and back another, in regard to

Beauty, but beauty of course was mingled with other things. I don't
Propose myself as a model. Far from that. Since I am still the
Same way, I am interested, though, in if how I am
Makes sense to me in the light of these other things I am saying.

One thing I notice I have done which does seem right to me
Is to think about beauty a good deal and see many examples
Of it, which has helped me to have what is called "good taste"
In it, so I am able to enjoy a great many things
That I otherwise could not have. Discriminating taste does not
Decrease the amount of beauty you perceive, but adds to it.
If you notice an opposite effect, you are "improving" in
The wrong way. Go visit a lot of foreign places
Where ordinary things have an extraordinary aspect and thus
Invite you to see them esthetically. Travel with someone
Else, and travel alone. Stand in front of a beautiful object until you
Are just about to feel tired of being there, then stop
And turn away. Vary your experience of what you see.
In variety is refreshment of the senses. A great painting, a
Mountain, and a person are a good combination for one day.
Sometimes, sameness increases beauty, or, rather,
Variety within sameness, as when looking at beautiful twins,
Triplets, or quadruplets, or in climbing a lot of staircases in Genoa,
A city famed for the beautiful structure of its stairways.

The impulse to "do something" about beauty
Can be acted on, as we have seen, by making love or, sometimes,
Even by marrying. Man is capable of improving
The beauty of nature in numerous ways, of which planting
Huge long rows of beautiful flowers is not the least. The
Cannas are nodding, the roses are asleep. And here's a
Tiny or medium-sized bumblebee, no it's a great big one!
And the oleanders are planted, they are standing
Next to the palms. You feel a surge of unaccountable delight. The wind
    moves them. And
Extraordinary cities may also be tucked together by
Human imaginations and hands. And other works of art as well.

Beauty is perceived in a curious way in poems,
Like the ocean seen through a partially knocked-down wall.
In music, beauty is "engaged in," as in sculpture and dance.

"I am beautiful, O mortals, like a dream of stone," says
Beauty, in Baudelaire's sonnet "La Beauté," where Baudelaire, in
Fewer words than I, has set down his ideas on the subject. Essentially he
Sees Beauty as eternal and pure, an enslaver of poets.
Rilke says that we love beauty because it "so serenely
Disdains to destroy us." In making works of art, then,
Is the excitement we feel that of being close to the elements of
Destruction? I do not want any mystery in this poem, so I will
Let that go. Or, rather, I want the mystery to be that it is clear
But says nothing which will satisfy completely but instead stirs to action
   (or contemplation)
As beauty does—that is, I wish it to be beautiful. But why I want that,
Even, I do not entirely know. Well, it would put it in a class of things
That seems the highest, and for one lifetime that should be enough.

Beauty is sometimes spoken of
As if it were a "special occasion," like going to the ballet
If one does that only once a year, or like going to
Church, if one does that only on religious holidays. Ex-
Perienced in this peripheral fashion, beauty cannot be
Sufficiently understood so as to be as valuable
To us as it should be, even if we do not understand it
Completely. Some understanding will rub off from frequent
Contact with it in both physical and intellectual ways,
And this understanding will do us some good. Of course,
It is possible to live without ever having seen mountains
Or the ocean, but it is not possible to live without having seen some
Beauty, and once one has seen something and
Liked it, one wants to have something more to do with
It, even to the point of having it inextricably tangled
Up with one's life, which beauty may be, anyway, whether we
Want it to be or not. It is a pleasure to be on top of things,
Even if only for a moment. Beauty may be an unsatisfiable

Appetite inducer, the clue to an infinite mystery, or a hoax,
Or perhaps a simple luxury for those with enough money and time
To go in pursuit of it, like châteaux vintages. Or it may be the whole works (see
Keats). It may simply be a bloom which is followed by
Fruition and not supposed to last and we have perversely arranged things
So in many cases it does, the way we force-feed geese
And pigs, and now we are simply stuck with it, grunting and
Cackling all around us, from which we try to make music.
Or it may be that beauty is an invitation
To a party that doesn't exist (Whitman thinks the party exists).
In any case, you will probably want as much
Of it as you can take with you, because it is, in spite of
All the doubts expressed above, certainly one of the sweetest things
In life. Of course, this is not the end of the subject, but it is
As far as I now can see, which in regard to beauty is
All we have, and one thing it seems to be about.

The Art of Love

"What do you know about it?"

I

To win the love of women one should first discover
What sort of thing is likely to move them, what feelings
They are most delighted with their lives to have; then
One should find these things and cause these feelings. Now
A story illustrates: of course the difficulty
Is how to talk about winning the love
Of women and not also speak of loving—a new
Problem? an old problem? Whatever—it is a something secret
To no one who has finally experienced it. Presbyopic. And so,
Little parks in Paris, proceed, pronounce
On these contributing factors to the "mental psyche
Of an airplane." Renumerate
The forces which gloss our tongues! And then Betty,
The youngest rabbit, ran, startled, out into the driveway,
Fear that Terry will run over her now calmed. Back
To the Alps, back to the love of women, the sunset
Over "four evenly distributed band lots in
Which you held my hand," mysterious companion
With opal eyes and oval face without whom I
Could never have sustained the Frogonian evening—
Wait a minute! if this is to be a manual of love, isn't it
Just about time we began? Well . . . yes. Begin.

Tie your girl's hands behind her back and encourage her
To attempt to get loose. This will make her breasts look
Especially pretty, like the Parthenon at night. Sometimes those
    illuminations
Are very beautiful, though sometimes the words
Are too expected, too French, too banal. Ain't youse a cracker,
Though? And other poems. Or Freemasonry Revisited. Anyway,
Tie her up. In this fashion, she will be like Minnie Mouse, will look
Like starlight over the sensuous Aegean. She will be the greatest thing
    you ever saw.
However, a word of advice, for cold September evenings,

And in spring, summer, winter too, and later in the fall:
Be sure she likes it. Or only at first dislikes it a little bit. Otherwise
You are liable to lose your chances for other kinds of experiments,
Like the Theseion, for example. Or the two-part song. Yes! this
Is Athens, king of the cities, and land of the
Countries of the Fall. Where *atoma* means person, and where was
A lovely epoch once though we however must go on
With contemporary problems in ecstasy. Let's see. Your
Girl's now a little tied up. Her hands stretched behind her at
An angle of about 40 degrees to her back, no, say, seventeen
And Z——sending his first roses at seventeen (roses also work
As well as hand tying but in a different less fractured
Framework) and she receiving them writing "I have never
Received roses before from a man. Meet me at the fountain
At nine o'clock and I will do anything you want." He was
Panicky! and didn't know what to do. What had he wanted
That now seemed so impossible? he didn't exactly know
How to do it. So he wrote to her that night amid the capitals
Of an arboring civilization, "Fanny I can't come. The maid is shocked.
     The
Butter factory is in an endzone of private feelings. So
The chocolate wasp stands on the Venetian steps. So
The cloudbursts are weeping, full of feeling
And stones, so the flying boats are loving and the tea
Is full of quotients. So—" That's enough cries Fanny she tears
It up then she reads it again. One breast may be somewhat higher
Than another with the hands tied behind. As Saint Ursula and her
     Virgins
Had the right attitude but were in the wrong field of fancy,
Not the sexual field, so these erogenous zones come
Forward when we need them if we are lucky and now I will speak
Of the various different virtues of rope, string, and chicken-wire—
If you want her to break loose suddenly in the middle
Of the lovemaking episode when you are inside her and cry yes
Yes throwing her arms and hands around you, then try string. Otherwise
     rope is most practical. As at Ravenna
The mosaics that start from the wall stay on the wall, in
The wall and they are the wall, in a sense, like the tracks in Ohio,

Pennsylvania, and Illinois. Rounding the bend you will see them.
They are hard to tell from the earth. She will kiss you then.

Thank you, parents of loving and passive girls, even a little bit
  masochistic ones
Who like the things this book is recommending. It is to you,
Although they do not know you often and
Even if they did might not consider this, men owe these joys.

To lack a woman, to not have one, and to be longing for one
As the grass grows around the Perrier family home,
That is the worst thing in life, but nowhere near the best is to have one
And not know what to do. So we continue these instructions.

The woman's feet may be tied as well as her hands. I'd suggest tying
  them
Or really the ankles, that's easier, to the legs at the foot of the bed
Or of the pool table if that is what you are making love upon. I
Remember a day in Paris when a man had a dancing bear
And I walked home to Freesia thinking about ape-mongering and death
  —Hold on a minute, there are
White blocks or cubes on the jetty of French poetic political
  involvement
Which "Love Does Not Need a Home" will cannily play for you on
  the phonograph
If you are not AC/DC ruining a certain part of the equipment. Her
  smile
Will be glorious, a sunrise, her feet tied to the legs of the bed.
If her hands are free she can move up and down readily (the
Sit up/lie down movement, near the Boulevard Raspail
And in irregular patterns—for some reason certain details
Keep coming back to undermine their candidacies). What good this will
  be to you
I don't know, but her sitting up and then lying down will (again)
Make her breasts look pretty (Fontainebleau you are my ark,
And Issy you are my loom!) and give tensity to the throat
Muscles and the stomach muscles too! You can simply enjoy that

(The tensing in the abdomen) by putting, lightly, your fingers on it (the
Abdomen) as one voyages on a Sunday to the Flea Market
Not in the hope of really finding anything but of sensing a new light
    panorama of one's needs.
So much for the pleasure in tensing stomach muscles. Of course with the
    girl tied this way
You can hit her up and down if you like to do that
And she will never be able to get up and walk away
Since she can't walk without her feet, and they are tied to the bed.

If you combine tying her hands to the bed and her feet
You can jump on her! She will be all flattened and splayed out.
What a fine way to spend an autumn afternoon, or an April one!
So delicious, you jumping up and down, she lying there, helpless,
    enjoying your every gasp!
You may enter her body at this point of course as well
As the Postal Museum stands only a few meterage yards away.
They have a new stamp there now, of a king with his crown
On backwards, dark red, it is a mistake, and worth five million pounds!
You can come out and go there, away! Dear, stay with me!!
And she pleads with you there as she lies on the bed, attached to the bed
By the cords you have tied with your hands, and attached to you by her
    love
As well, since you are the man who attached her there,
Since you are the knowing lover using information gleaned from this
    volume.

Tying up, bouquets, bouqueting bunch-of-flowers effects. Tie her hands
    and legs
Together, I mean her hands and feet, I mean ankles. There are different
    processes.
Tie the left hand to the left ankle, right hand to right ankle.
Spread out in any position and make love. She will be capable of fewer
    movements
But may bring you a deep-sea joy. Crabs and lobsters must love like that
And they don't stay down at the bottom of the ocean for nothing—
It must be wonderful! In any case you can try it in your mistress's bed

Or in your own of course. You can tie left hand to right ankle
And so on. This gives a criss-cross effect
And is good after a quarrel. The breasts in all these cases look
Exceptionally beautiful. If you do not like liking
These breasts so much you may hit them
If she likes that, and ask her to ask you to hit them, which
Should increase your pleasure in mastery particularly if she is all tied up.
"Hit My Tits" could be a motto on the sailboat of your happiness. If
    you don't think
You have gotten your money's worth already
From this book you deserve to turn in an early grave
Surrounded by worm women who assail and hit you
Until there is nothing left of you so hard that they can't eat.
But I am sure this is not your feeling. So, having agreed,
Let us go on. You should buy another book
And give it to your best friend, however, if at this point you do agree
    with me.
I will wait; meanwhile we can both stare at your mistress, where she is
    all tied up.

Well, you can roll her like a wheel, though I doubt she'll approve of it,
Women rarely do, I knew one once, though, who did. For
This of course you use the right hand right ankle left
Hand left ankle arrangement, using splints on both sides of each
Knot so that the limbs will stay in wheel-position. Now that she
Looks like that which makes a chariot roll, roll her! If this hurts her,
Soothe her a little by kissing her all around, saying
"Ah, my lovely wheel, went over a bump, did it?" and so on,
Until she finally is resigned to being your wheel, your dear beloved one
And is eager to be rolled about by you. Small objects placed on the
    floor
Will give you brief twinges of sadistic energy and speed up your
    wheeling.
I suggest ending by wheeling her out an opened door
Which you then close and stab yourself to death. This procedure,
    however, is rare.

I was carried away. Forgive me. The next chapters will be much more
   sane.

Nailing a woman to the wall causes too much damage
(Not to the wall but to the woman—you after all want to enjoy her
And love her again and again). You can, however, wrap tape around her
   arms, waist, ankles, and knees
And nail this to the wall. You'll enjoy the pleasure of nailing
And the very thought of it should make her scream. You can fit this
   tape
On her like tabs, so your girl will be like a paper doll.
And you can try things on her once she is nailed up. You can also
Throw things at her, which is something I very much like to do—
Small rakes, postal scales, aluminum belt buckles, Venetian glass
   clowns—
As soon as you start to hurt her, you should stop
And kiss her bruises, make much of them, draw a circle around each hit
With a bold felt pen. In this way you can try to hit the same spots over
   and over again
As the little park grows larger the more you look at it
But the flowers are in another story, a lemon-covered volume, stop! The
   knees
Of this girl are now looking very pretty, so go and kiss them
And slip your hands around the back of them and feel what is called
The inside of the knee and tell her you love her.
If she is able to talk she will probably ask you to take her down,
Which you then can do. However, if she wants to stay up there
As blue day changes to night, and is black in the hemispheres, and boats
   go past
And you are still feeling wonderful because of her beautiful eyes
And breasts and legs, leave her there and run up against her
As hard as you can, until the very force of your bumping
Breaks tape from nail or girl from tape or breaks great chunks of wall
So you and she lie tumbled there together
Bruises on her body, plaster on your shoulders, she bloody, she
   hysterical, but joy in both your hearts.
Then pull off the tape if it hasn't come off

And bite her to the bone. If she bites you back, appoint her
"Lover" for a while and let her do all this to you. That is,
If you'd like it. You'll suffer, of course, from being less beautiful than
    she
And less soft, less inviting to cause pain to. To be a great lover,
However, you must be a great actor, so try, at least once.

Oh the animals moving in the stockyards have no idea of these joys
Nor do the birds flying high in the clouds. Think: tenderness cannot be
    all
Although everyone loves tenderness. Nor violence, which gives the sense
    of life
With its dramas and its actions as it is. Making love must be
    everything—
A city, not a street; a country, not a city; the universe, the world—
Make yours so, make it even a galaxy, and be conscious and unconscious
    of it all. That is the art of love.

2

Which cannot be begun, however, until you meet somebody
You want to make love to, a subject to be dealt with in these chapters.
So, avanti! Here you are, girl-less, wandering the city's streets
Or deep in the country, pale amid flowers, or staring, perhaps too!,
At barrels of camel dung being shoved down a road in the Middle East
Or on a skyscraper in a great city, ten thousand miles beneath the ocean
    floor,
How do you meet a woman? or, if you like younger women, a girl?
Well, the thing to do is find out where local girls congregate—
This may be at the camel shack, along the shore of the Ashkenazi or the
    Mediterranean
At a beach, or along the side streets or at the school, wherever
It is, go there! You will be happy once you have seen the girls
Or women and your body becomes active, reminding you you must
    succeed
As the earthquake and the volcano remind life they must succeed

And it must succeed. Success is a joy although it is not everything—
Still, in matters of love, there is nothing without it! With no
Success, simply nothing happens. You are a dead person in a field
With mud being heaped on you; without success,
Nothing happens in the field of love. Something
Has to be there, a spark, a firm handclasp, a meaningful look, some
    hope,
Something, which one can get only in the presence of women
Since if they are not there, how can they give it? But
You do not need to be reminded of this, you are already reading
This strangely eventful and staggering "Art of Love."

Many people get married before they even realize how to meet girls
And so have a wide selection; this may result in infidelity, divorce,
And frustrated feelings; so it is a good idea, whether you are
    contemplating marriage or not,
To learn where to meet, to find the women whom you might love.
In big cities often guidebooks are accurate indications
Of some of the spots to begin your search. Great tourist attractions
Such as the Acropolis, the Bermuda Shorts factory, and St. Peters in
    Rome
Are likely to attract women as well as men, since they too share such
    human feelings
As curiosity, interest, the desire to find "something afar
From the sphere of our sorrow" (as Shelley says), always hoping to find
    this,
Even as men are, in some storied successes of history, business, or art.
So that is a good place to meet them, too, since their souls are likely to
    be open
In a way they are not otherwise: historical beauty is a friend,
Opening and softening the feelings, but no human friend is there,
So you may fill the gap by sharing the openness with her,
And by appreciating the work at hand. Some like to fall down right
    there
And "made love my first sight of the Acropolis" or
"Bellini's pictures moved me, so—" As the ferry boat
Pursues its course from Brindisi to Corfu and back again

Many young couples were seen steaming on its decks
With happy energy, and among the lime trees in Southern Africa
A thousand hippopotamuses met with glee and frightened everyone away
By their lovemaking, which increased the acidity of the limes
One million per cent. Why should they be having all the fulfilment and
    fun
And you not? My friends, there is no reason. So another kind of place
    to go
In cities is the college restaurants. There young girls congregate speaking
    of their courses
And their boyfriends and their professors. You can pretend to be a poet
Or a professor, and speak to them about starting a little shop
Where no one will come. Their curiosity piqued, they may follow you
    as far as a coffee shop
Where you can go on speaking to them, in private—but that is covered
    in
The next chapter—"Antic," or "What to Say." Sometimes a department
    store
Will be full of women. You can go as a woman yourself, as a
Cripple who needs their help, or as a regular man shopping for some
    real woman he knows
Who needs their advice. It doesn't matter how you go; what matters
Is getting the woman alone, so you can speak of your desires.
No one can resist this, but first you have to find the one to speak to.
Well, almost no one—but your ratio anyway should be seven to one,
Success over failure. Dangerous intersections in mid-city
Are good places to meet girls and help them across the street.
You can stand there and do this all day, madly dodging the traffic
And with a happy smile you find the one you like and cross her too
With a swift hit on the belly and a large and wicked smile.
She will look at you surprised and you can carry on from there, but at
    least you will be beginning
With her grateful to you, for having steered her across the street.

Life is full of horrors and hormones and so few things are certain,

So many unknown—but the pleasure of coupling with a creature one is
   crazy about
Is something undisputed. So don't be afraid to spend
Hours, even days, weeks, even months, going to places
And trying to find the person who can give you the maximum pleasure
   in life
As the sun hits the top of mountains but often prefers the hills
Where markets glint in the fading light and one's lungs seem filled with
   silver. O horrors of loneliness!
Abandon my spirit while it walks forth through the world and attempts
   to find for people
And tell them where marvelous women can be found. Of course, you
   want a very particular one.
To find her, however, you may have to look at a great many, and try
   more,
Some in the light, some in the dark. Orgies are sometimes organized for
   people,
You can try that, but I wouldn't, all life is an
Orgy, why limit oneself to a little room, full of (probably)
Mainly people who are emotionally disturbed
As you and I are not. If you could organize an orgy
Of your own, that might, I think, be something else. But
We have strayed from our subject. The Cross of the Seven Winds Hotel
On East Vortex Street, in Albenport, is a good place to meet girls,
It so happens there are always a tremendous number of them there
(No one has ever known why). And there you may find someone!

Happy the man who has two breasts to crush against his bosom,
A tongue to suck on, a lip to bite, and in fact an entire girl! He knows
   a success
Not known by Mount Aetna or Vesuvius or by any major volcano of
   the world!
He has someone to come into, and stay there and tremble, and shake
   about, and hold,
And dream about, and come back to, and even discuss party politics with
   if he wants to,

Or poetry, or painting. But where shall you find this bird? On a
  gondola in Venice
The tour guide said, "Look at those buildings" and I felt my chest
  crushed against your
Bosom, and the whole earth went black; when I awoke we were in
  Brindisi,
You had nailed me to a canoe, you were standing on my stomach, you
  had a rat in your hand
Which you were waving in the summer breeze, and saying "This is
  from the Almanach
Of Living, attention, please pay attention, greeniness and mountains, oh
  this is the art of love!"

Uncooperative cities! your hideous buildings block out air and sunlight!
  Fumes
Destroy human lungs! Muggers and burglars
Infest your streets! You're horrible! I hate you! (Sometimes.) Where else
  are women to be found
And the sweet joys they furnish, the prospect of a life joined to a life
More wonderful than air joined to a fountain—there is nothing like the
  art of love!
A plume, a cabana, a canvas, a modern tire, a pampa, a plume, a sailboat
All have meaning as an ocean has tar, in relation to love only. Yes,
That's my secret. What is yours? I mean to say without love everything
  is only half in order,
Or two-fifths, or one-third, perhaps for many and I think I am one
Hardly ordered at all, for us, without love, life is a great mess! By order
  I mean clarity, I mean joy.

In India the art of love has been studied in great detail
But that was in another age, another time. My book brings it all up to
  date
And is oriented to the Western World! Though my Chinese edition
May soon be forthcoming!
But now off to the country! And how there to find girls!

Sometimes in the country there may actually be no girls
And one must return disconsolately to the city. However, first one
    should have a good and intensive look,
For to fail, and especially in matters of love, is depressing
And depression eats the heart away and makes one less able to love.
Oysters, clams, steak, anything with a high protein content
Is good for one's sexual powers, since semen is all protein;
For the feeling part, self-confidence, joy, and a tender and passionately
    loving heart!
How can girls stay away from you? They will have to find you
If you are like that! But what if they do not know you exist?

So—in the country, WALK! circulate, cover as many square inches of
    the area as you can
So that female eyes can see you, even if they are hidden behind ramparts
    of hay
Or cow barriers, pig barriers, hog barriers, chicken barriers, bull barriers,
Even peering out from between the interstices of a barn. Once they see
    you
They will love you, if your radiance shines in your face
(For this there are chemical preparations, but naturalness is best)
And they will tentatively come out to meet you. Here, immediate
    love-making is best
Because of lack of places to go, chance of the angry farmer, etcetera,
But this may be dealt with later. In Turkey, in the country,
Sling your girl under a camel, and have her there. You will thrill gently
And greatly as the camel trots down the road toward the mill,
Where you will be thrown amidst the raw grain. You must immediately
    escape
Or you'll be ground to bits! And take the girl off with you
For she may later come to be the one that you will love,
Which you cannot do if she is in a thousand pieces, or even in fifteen
Or three. One man once loved a girl who was in two
But that was a rare occasion and does not affect the more general
    behavior
That is the subject of this book. So rescue the girl. In any case,

149

Even if you do not love her later, you will, I feel sure,
Enjoy making love that once after escaping from death.

For meeting girls, then, in the country, the rule is BE SEEN.
In the city, GO WHERE THEY ARE. In Turkey, or any foreign
    country,
TRAVEL WITH THEIR CUSTOMS OF LIFE, as with the incident
    of the camel.
Having found the woman, however, what can you say?

Or what if she runs past you, fleetingly, at the beginning of night?

3

Of course you must stop her. Say anything: "Hello!" "Good-bye!"
Anything to arrest her attention, so that when her pace is slowed
She will be able to listen to you and be totally entranced by you,
So that later she will be with you, all breasts and fragrance!
And what you say should not merely win over the woman
But add to the zest and to the glory of everything you do.

Sweet is making love out of doors, and making love on walls
Built to surround ancient cities, sweet being close to a girl beneath
    overhead highways
Or in a downtown sunlit hotel, from which afterwards you walk out
    and look at the statues
Of the city, at the main piazza, and the opera dome. And sweet it is if
    you have engraved your name
Or written it or stamped it on your girl's thigh, to walk on mirrored
    floors
So you can see it. And it is a great pleasure
To have your girl riding on a wagon and you run after her
And catch her and pull her down and make love on the road in the
    dust.
Sweet the first contact of bodies—and one of the sweetest things in life
    is to talk to someone

Delicious and unavailable and to wholly win her over by what you say!

When you first see a woman you do not know, some time, some
  autumn, Septembery
Day when the leaves are making curtains through which the gargoyles
  peer
At you as you are standing there astonished by that ivory and those
  hooks
You imagine to be holding all together without which she would be
  naked and in your arms,
As you stand there thinking of that, you may find yourself speechless
From so much excitement! In such situations, one
Thing you can usually rely on is asking for directions—
To someplace, to be sure, which you cannot find unless she goes with
  you,
And of course you should have some room along the way
To which you can take her. And it is a good idea in most cases also
To ask for directions to places that are likely to excite the
Woman you are asking them of, such as "Where is the Duomo of
  Ropes?" or
"In what museum is the Daumier painting of the girl who is rolling like
  a wheel?"

If you pretend a woman is someone you already know,
An already existing girlfriend, lost love, former student, and so on, that
  is also a good way to
Begin, and you can start in talking at once in a relaxed and
Intimate way, which is a joy in itself. And if you pretend to know a
  woman, you can kiss her
At once, which is always an excellent idea. Not only does doing so
Sometimes bring instant success, but it also prepares the way
For possible future encounters, as does thoughtful praise—
For a well-placed compliment, like an Easter egg, beautiful but hidden,
Can influence a woman, as a kiss can, for years of her life.

In general, you should kiss as many women as you can,
Taking any excuse to do so: pretending you know her, saying

Hello or good-bye to her, seeing her at a parade, at a party, and so on.
In train stations, kiss any pretty girl in sight. A friendly kiss may
    implant in a girl the idea
That she would like to see you again. Then who knows what may
    happen?

Compliments may be whispered as the girl walks past you;
Stated to her directly, as you move into her path, then bow as she goes
    by you;
Read into a dictaphone and played as woman after woman comes
    along.
They may be given when you do not know the woman; given after one
    minute's acquaintance;
After two; after three. The "striking" compliment, i.e., with which
    to
Win the one one does not know should not be delayed beyond
    approximately
Three minutes, unless some other potent factor is having an effect—your
Being famous, excessively good-looking, or covered with precious jewels
Or being accompanied by an interesting gigantic animal, i.
E., anything that will make talk easy because of astonishment
Or admiration—but even in these cases you should quickly come to
    praise
Because it is so moving, and love makes it so natural a thing to do.

In regard to content, compliments are of six types, reducible to three
Chief ones, which are Compliments to the Body—including of course
    the face,
The coloration, and the movements; Compliments to the Mind—for
Lack of a better term, considered to include the sensibility
As a whole, sensitivity in particular, deep understanding, and
Comprehension of details; and Compliments to Something Else—
    whatever
Doesn't go in One or Two, such as ability to fire clay sculptures,
    arrange flowers,
Or behavior and elegance in general. Under this last could come

Moral or characterological praise, though this might be considered as
    being in Category Two.
The essence of the compliment, of whatever type it is
You give the woman, if it is to give you the maximum
Benefits of her enjoyment and passion for you, and if you are to
Like giving it, as one may like giving the world a poem,
A symphony, or a bridge, is that it be free, a free possession
Of the woman or girl that you give it to, in other words that she
Feels no obligation to respond (though I assure you that she will)
And feels free to wear it entirely on her own. Then she will turn to you
With happy and returning desire. Of all compliments there
Are two kinds: those which show desire, and those which do not. "You
    look Etruscan!"
Is a good example of the compliment without desire
(Apparently) and "You look so delicious I want to bite you! My God,
    you drive me
Crazy!" is an example of the other kind. In the one case the woman is
    left with
A high historic feeling and feeling her beauty is somehow eternal,
That she shares in an eternally beautiful type
Away from the sphere of our sorrow, and thus that her life must
    somehow mean something
And she be an achievement of some marvelous kind (which she is), and
    the other, more
Earthy-seeming compliment makes her feel a happy object of desire,
The source of fervid feeling in others, a sort of springtide or passage of
    time,
Or else a Venus, or else a sunrise, or sunset, the cause of sleepless
    evenings and gasps
(This compliment is not demanding, because it is exaggerated
And humorous in being that, and lets the woman decide).

Everything about love makes people feel in a more intense way,
So it seems natural enough to start right in, with "You are beautiful
As a) Botticelli's Venus, or b) a slice of angelfood cake, I want
To devour you—for my sweet tooth is the ruling tooth of my life!"

153

Later you can cry to her, when alone with her, "Oh you are the
    enslaving of me,
Dear sweet and irrefutable love!" And when you are dancing with her
Or anywhere in public, you may even wish to praise her
In a secret language which no one else will understand—
"Gah shlooh lye bopdoosh," for example, may mean "Your left leg
Is whiter even than the snow which on Mount Kabanayashi
Tops all Japan with its splendor!" And "Ahm gahm doom bahm
    ambahm glahsh": "I
Would like to tie you to this bannister and
Kill you with my kisses all night!" For if you believe
There is a magic in love, to get to it you will go to any extremes.

And one goes on looking, and talking. And neither the tongue
Nor the eyes wear out, and the streets are filled with beautiful breasts
    and words.

One excellent thing to do once a woman will listen to you
Is to read her poems, and the best of all poems to read is this one,
Accompanied, if you like, by acting out its details. Which now let us
    continue.

    4

For there are numerous questions remaining which one must consider
If one is serious about love and determined to learn all its ways.

What is Love's Ideal City? what strange combination
Of Paris and Venice, of Split for the beauty of its inhabitants,
Of Waco for its byways, of Vladivostok for its bars?
What, precisely, is meant by the "love of God"? or the "love of
    humanity"?
How can girls best be conquered in different cities?
What places, or bits of landscape, most speak of love?
How to make your girlfriend into an airplane, or a living kite;
How to convert success in business or art into success in love;

Keeping one's libidinous impulses at a peak all the time;

How to explain, and how to prosper with having two loves, or three, or four, or five;

Meeting women, disguised, in museums, and walking with them, naked, in the country;

How to speak of love when you do not know the language; how to master resentment;

How to cause all the women eating in a given restaurant to fall in love with you at the same time;

Greek aphrodisiac foods, how to eat them and how to prepare them;

One secret way to make any woman happy she is with you;

Apollo: woman-chaser, homosexual, or both? Zeus: godlike ways of seducing women;

How to judge the accuracy of what you remember about past love;

Building a house ideally suited to love; how to reassure virgins;

How to avoid being interested in the wrong woman; seven sure signs of someone you don't want to love;

Three fairly reliable signs of someone you do;

Use of the car—making love under the car; in the car; on the car roof;

Traveling with women; what to do when suddenly you know that the whole relationship is no longer right;

How to pump fresh air into the lungs of a drowned girl; the "kiss of death"; how to appear totally confident and totally available for love at the same time;

Maintaining good looks under exhausting conditions; forty-one things to think about in bed;

How to win the love of a girl who is half your age; how to win the love of one who is one fifth your age;

Bracelets women like to have slipped onto them; places in which women are likely to slip and thus fall into your arms;

The bridge of ships: how to make love there in twenty-five different positions

So as to have a happy and rosy complexion later, at the "Captain's Table";

Love in different cultures: how to verify what you are feeling in relation to the different civilizations of the world—

155

Room for doubt: would the Greeks have called this "love"? Do such
  feelings exist in China?
Did they exist in Ming China? And so on. The Birthday of Love—
On what day is Eros's birthday correctly celebrated? Was love born only
  once?
Is there actually a historical date? Presents to give on such a day;
What memorable thing did Spinoza say about love? How to deal with
  the sweethearts of your friends
When they want to go to bed with you; how to make love while
  asleep;
The Book of Records, and what it says; how to end a quarrel;
How to plan a "day of love"—what food and drink to have by your
  side, what newspapers and books;
How to propose the subject so that your girlfriend will go away with
  you
On a "voyage to the moon," i.e., lie under the bed while you
Create a great hole in the mattress and springs with your hatchet
And then leap on her, covered with feathers and shiny metal spring
Fragments, screaming, as you at last make love, "We are on the moon!"
  How to dress
Warmly for love in the winter, and coolly in the sun;
Mazes to construct in which you can hide naked girls and chase them;
Dreams of love, and how they are to be interpreted;
How "love affairs" usually get started; when to think of marriage; how
  to prevent your girl from marrying someone else;
"Magical feelings"—how to sustain them during a love affair; traveling
  with a doctor
As a way to meet sick girls; traveling with a police officer as a way to
  meet criminal girls;
What is "Zombie-itis"? do many women suffer from it? how can it be
  enjoyed
Without actually dying? where are most adherents to it found?
What ten things must an older man never say to a young woman?
What about loving outdoors? what good can we get there from trees,
  stones, and rivers?
Are there, in fact, any deities or gods of any kind to Love?
And if so, can they be prayed to? Do the prayers do any good?

What can be done to cure the "inability to love"? senseless promiscuity?
twenty-four-hour-a-day masturbatory desires?
What nine things will immediately give anyone the power to make
love?
What three things must usually be forgotten in order to make love?
Ways of leaving your initial on girls; other "personalizing insignia";
How to turn your girl into a duck, turkey, or chicken, for fifteen
minutes;
What to do when she comes back to herself, so she will not be angry or
frightened;
How to make love while standing in the sea; cures for "frozen legs";
Love's icebox;
Love Curses to blight those who interfere with you, and Love Charms
to win those who resist you;
Traveling while flat on your back; Girls from Sixteen Countries; what to
do with a Communist or other Iron-Curtain-Country Girl
So that politics will not come into it, or will make your pleasure even
greater;
How to identify yourself, as you make love, with sunlight, trees, and
clouds;
What to do during a Sex Emergency: shortage of girls, lack of desire,
absence of space in which to sit or lie down;
How to really love a woman or girl for the rest of your life; what to
do if she leaves you;
Seventeen tried and tested cures for the agonies of lost love;
Telling a "true" emotion from an in some way "untrue" one;
How to compensate for being too "romantic"; can enjoyed love ever
come up to romantic expectations?
Ways of locating women who love you in a crowd; giving in totally to
love;
How to transform a woman into a "Human Letter"
By covering her with inscriptions, which you then ship to yourself
In another bedroom, unwrap it, read it, and make love;
Making love through a piece of canvas; making love through walls;
What to do when one lover is in a second-floor apartment, the other in
the first-floor one;

Openings in the ceiling, and how to make them; how to answer the
   question
"What are you doing up there on the ceiling?" if someone accidentally
   comes home;
Ways to conceal the fact that you have just made love or
Are about to make love; how to explain pink cheeks, sleepiness.
Is love all part of a "Great Plan," and, if so, what is the Plan?
If it is to keep the earth populated, then what is the reason behind that?
Throwing your girl into the ocean and jumping in after her, aphrodisiac
   effects of; genius,
Its advantages and disadvantages in love; political antagonism in love:
She is a Moslem, you are a Republican; or she is a Maoist, and you are
   for improving the system;
How to keep passion alive while beset by anxiety and doubt;
What is the best way to make love in a rocket? what is the second-best
   way?
How to make sure one's feeling is "genuine"; how to use gags; when to
   wear a hat;
At what moment does drunkenness become an impediment to love?
What is the role of sex in love? Is fidelity normal? Are all women, in
   one sense, the same woman?
How can this best be explained to particular women? Drawing one's
   portrait on a woman's back—
Materials and methods; is growing older detrimental to love?
Use of the aviary; use of the kitchen garden; what are eighteen totally
   unsuspected enemies of love?
Does lack of love "dry people up"? how can one be sure one's love will
   be lasting?
What reasonable substitute, in love's absence, could be found for love?

The best authors to consult about love (aside from the author of this
Volume) are Ovid, Ariosto, Spenser, and Stendhal. Places or bits of
   landscape
Which most speak of love: Piazzale Michelangelo, looking down at the
   Arno, above Florence;
The candy factory in Biarritz, specializing in ruby-red hearts;
Gus's Place, in Indonesia, a small cart-wheel store full of white paper;
   the Rotterdam Harbor on an April evening.

The Ideal City for Love—should be a combination
Of Naples, for its byways and its population and its Bay; Paris,
For everything except the stinginess of some of its inhabitants;
Rome, for its amazement, not for its traffic; Split, for its absence of the
    Baroque;
Austin, Texas, for having so many pretty girls there; Eveningtown,
    Pennsylgrovia, for being completely unknown,
So no one can come in to spoil the lovification, although many can and
    do come in
And are swept up into it entirely, I will tell you later, if I remember,
    how to get there;
Shanghai, for the unusability of its streets; Hangkow, for its evenings;
    Phoenix, for its temperature
On autumn evenings; Mexico City, for its Fragonardesque rose
Of bullfights! the caped hat! the paseos! And the magic Aspirin tablet of
    Capesville, Georgia,
Where no one lives; Easter Island City, for the uncloistered quality of its
    inhabitants; Thailand Chonk,
For the bittersweet lemons sold at its fair; and Egg-Head, Florida, for its
    stones.
This ideal city of love will not be as spread out
As London is, or as over-towering as New York, but it will be a city.
    Suburbs are inimical to love,
Imposing the city's restrictions without its stimulation and variety.
The city must include numerous girls. Therefore city planners
Will include as many colleges as they can and encourage
Such professions as will draw young women to the city from outside.

To make your girl into an airplane, ask her to lie down on a large piece
    of canvas
Which you have stretched out and nailed to a thin sheet of aluminum,
    or, if you are economizing, of balsa wood.
When she has lain down, wrap the stuff she is lying on around her
And ask her to stretch out her arms, for these will be the wings
Of the plane (she should be lying on her stomach), with her neck
    stretched taut, her chin
Resting on the canvas (her head should be the "nose" of the plane); her
    legs and feet should be

Close together (tied or strapped, if you like). Now, once she is in
   airplane position,
Wrap the aluminum or balsa-coated canvas more closely around her and
   fasten it at the edges
With staples, glue, or rivets. Carry her to the airport, or to any
   convenient field,
And put her on the ground. Ask her to "take off!" If she does, you have
   lost a good mistress. If not
(And it is much more likely to be "if not"), you will enjoy making
   love there on the field—
You, both pilot and crew, and passengers, and she your loving plane!

Perhaps you would also like to turn your girl into a shoe or into a
   shoebox
Or a plaster cherry tree or any one of a million other things. A booklet
   is coming out
Specifically and entirely on that, called *The Shop of Love*.

The best way to conquer girls in different cities is to know the mayor or
   ruler of the particular city
And have him introduce you to the girls (perhaps while they are under
   the influence of a strong love-making drug).

To revive an old love affair, write the woman concerned, or call her up.
   Suggest converting her into a plane.
If she loves you still, she'll hesitate or say yes. If she says no, propose
   converting her into the summer dawn.

To cause all the women in a given restaurant to wish to make love to
   you,
Bring in the model of an airplane and stare at it attentively and refuse to
   eat.

You can tell a woman's character by looking in her shoe, if you have
   the special glasses described in *The Shop of Love*.
Otherwise, the eyes, mouth, and breasts are better indications.

If the breasts are round, she may be foolish; if the eyes are green, she
    may be Jewish;
If the mouth is full, she may be pettish. But everything she is will be
    for you.

The wrong woman can be identified by the following characteristics:
She eats at least twice as much as you do; her shoes or clothing are
    unbuttoned or untied; she dislikes cold water;
Her face is the shape of a donkey's; she fears evening
For evening draws one closer to bed. She contradicts herself
And is stubborn about each thing she said. She is perpetually unhappy
And would hate you bitterly for changing her condition. Immediately
    leave her! This person is not for you!

Two signs of love-worthiness in a woman are climbing to the roof
Without fear and with a smile on her face; turning around to look at
    you after she turns away from you.

Use of the car is now located in *The Shop of Love.*

When you know the relationship is not right, think of it all again.
Try again the next day. If you still think the same thing, end it.

The kiss of death is currently prohibited by law. Look for it in later
    editions.

To maintain good looks under exhausting conditions, think about an
    eskimo
Riding a white horse through a valley filled with falling other eskimos
So that he always has to be attentive, so that no eskimo falls on his
    head.
This will give you an alert look, which is half of beauty.

One thing to think about in bed is the full extent of this poem.
Another is the city of Rome. Another is the Byzantine stained-glass
    window showing Jesus as a human wine-press.

Do not think of cancellation of air trips, botched tennis racquets, or
 slightly torn postage stamps.
Think of the seasons. Think of evening. Think of the stone duck
Carved by the cement company in Beirut, to advertise
Their product. Think of October. Do not think of sleep.

To win the love of a girl half your age, add your age and hers together
And divide by two; act as if you were the age represented by that
 number
And as if she were too; the same with girls one fourth or one fifth your
 age.
This is called "Age Averaging," and will work in all those cases
In which age difference is a problem. Often it is not.

Love between living beings was unknown in Ming China. All passion
 was centered on material things.
This accounts for the vases. In Ancient Greece there was no time for
 love. In Somaliland only little children love each other.

Spinoza's remark was "Love is the idea of happiness attached to an
 external cause."

Friends' sweethearts should be put off until the next day.

To make love while asleep, try reading this book. It has been known to
 cause Somnamoria.

The Book of Records says the record number of times a man made love
 in a twenty-four-hour period was 576 times.
The record number of times a woman made love was 972 times.
The man died, and the woman went to sleep and could not be awakened
 for two years.
She later became the directress of a large publishing house and then later
 in life became a nun.
The most persons anyone ever made love to in rapid succession (without
 a pause of any kind) was seventy-one.

Dreams about love should be acted on as quickly as possible
So as to be able to fully enjoy their atmosphere. If you dream about a
woman, phone her at once and tell her what you have dreamed.

Zombie-itis is love of the living dead. It is comparatively rare.
If a woman likes it, you can probably find other things she likes that
you will like even more.

Ten things an older man must never say to a younger woman:
1) I'm dying! 2) I can't hear what you're saying! 3) How many fingers
are you holding up?
4) Listen to my heart. 5) Take my pulse. 6) What's your name?
7) Is it cold in here? 8) Is it hot in here? 9) Are you in here?
10) What wings are those beating at the window?
Not that a man should stress his youth in a dishonest way
But that he should not unduly emphasize his age.

The inability to love is almost incurable. A long sea voyage
Is recommended, in the company of an irresistible girl.

To turn a woman into a duck, etc., hypnotize her and dress her in
costume.
To make love standing in water, see "Elephant Congress" in the *Kama
Sutra* (chap. iv).
During a shortage of girls, visit numerous places; give public lectures;
carry this volume.

Lost love is cured only by new love, which it usually makes impossible.
Finding a girl who resembles the lost girl may offer temporary relief.

One test for love is whether at the beginning you are or are not able to
think about anything else.

To locate unknown-about love for you in a woman in a crowd,
Look intently at everyone you find attractive, then fall to the ground.
She will probably come up to you and show her concern.

Railway Express will not handle human letters, but Bud's Bus and
   Truck Service will.

Sleepiness may be explained by drugs; pink cheeks, by the allergy that
   caused you to take them.

Love being part of a Great Plan is an attractive idea
But has never been validated to anyone's complete satisfaction.

Throwing your girl in the ocean makes her feel sexy when she gets out.
   Genius is not a disadvantage.

Hats should never be worn when making love. All women are not the
   same woman
Though they may sometimes seem so. The aviary is best used on summer
   nights. There is no
Substitute for or parallel to love, which gives to the body
What religion gives to the soul, and philosophy to the brain,
Then shares it among them all. It is a serious matter. Without it, we
   seem only half alive.

May good fortune go with you, then, dear reader, and with the women
   you love.

from

The Burning Mystery of Anna in 1951

Our Hearts

I

All hearts should beat when Cho Fu's orchestra plays "Love"
And then all feet should start to move in the dance.
The dancing should be very quick and all step lightly.
Everyone should be moving around, all hearts beating—
Tip tap tip tap. The heart is actually beating all the time
And with almost the same intensity. The difference is not in our hearing
Which is also almost always the same. The difference must be really,
Then, in our consciousness, which, they say, is variegated.
Black-and-white shoes, red dress, an eye of flame,
A teeth of pearl, a hose of true, a life of seethings. Would
You like to dance? The excitement, it is there all the time.
Is human genius there all the time? With the analogy of dreams,
Which supposedly we have every night, one is tempted
To say, The seething is always there, and with it the possibility for great
    art.

2

The government is there all the time, or actually the people
Struggle first so the government will be there then so it will not
Be overpowering. When does the art come, and the seething,
And when is the best point for justice, in all these I would like to be
    living.
The houses come and then the industry and then the people
And the government must control the industry. No smoke in the houses.
And there are people who study this all the time,
Economists, government people, they sit down and walk about
And study these things. And some otherwise indistinguishable boys
And girls become scientists, and complicate these things,
Make them better and worse, and some pale insecure others
Come along and do poems and paintings, and all die
And new ones are born, and there gets to be history and culture
And civilization and the death of civilization and the life of it and in it.

3

We, who are born in it, walk around in it, and look at these things
And think of these things. Some things are first and some are second.
No one has yet completely figured out our brain
But some are trying. One of the first things is we try to be "all right,"
To do well and to succeed. Whether this is in all human brains
(We think not) or only in our civilization's, we don't know
For sure, or much care, but we act by it anyway, just as we act
By the morality we happen to be born with (i.e., not eating our
     grandparents
As Herodotus said the Egyptians thought it proper to do).
And in the dim, dazzling adolescent ballrooms we start on our way.
Later, much later perhaps, we try to figure it out—
Or sometimes just start working mechanically on one aspect.
Finding ourselves "in love," we may attach supreme value to that
Or to some crazy religion, finding ourselves in a church at sunset.

4

What do you think it is really all explainable by, this
Mystery that has been built up by a natural process
And how much of it do we need? The foot of everyone is advancing
And the knees of everyone should be flexing, legs dancing
And lips moving gaily up over the teeth
For the speaking, and hands driven into the pockets, eyes shining, stub-
bed toes forgotten as we walk down the somewhere else saying God
     Damn
It's good to see you. But what shall we do? The greatest plan
Is participate, aid, and understand. Every dog should be at the foot
Of every man. What evidence this past give us! Examples
With which we impregnate today. But the shirt should fit
Over the chest, the light silk panties over the rear.
The sky is shining. The sun is a basket of wash
Let down for our skin, and germs are all around us like cash.

5

In nature is no explanation. In city is no
Explanation. In language is no
Explanation. Explanation is a dog, is a languishing lad
Lanky with lurid binoculars, dilapidated-looking. I am
Sitting and you are standing. We have a knowledge of good and bad.
I am exploding with doubts and with talent. I look everywhere.
I'm always glad when I find something simple.
Breathing is simple, walking is simple, and dancing, sometimes, moving
    one's feet.
A simple way to say that things are simple
Is immensely enjoyable but it is not explanation.
The people should be rushing along. There is in that way no problem
Except there is this problem How to participate aid and understand
Simultaneously. It seems there is too much. Participating in the wall
You forget to understand the tax reform. And aid no one.

6

So what is the ecstasy we are allowed to have in this one life
As everybody says that we are getting on with living here?
Should you devote your life to reform? or to understanding your life?
Are different kinds of people born, some for aiding,
Some for participating in, some for understanding life?
Which one are you and how do you know? You are crazy
And don't know it, one person says, and another says, You are asleep.
To myself I seem sane and awake, and I go on.
Maybe a fundamental-type solution, "loss in nature," "mystical religion"
Or "sexual explosiveness" is what we need. But dear civilization—
Who would like to give up theater for climbing up a tree? No one
    wants you to.
Remember where this meditation began (with Cho Fu's orchestra).
It is the problem of living and not being the first one
And yet wanting to do as much as that first one, and, because there is all
    that train behind one, more.

7

The people look at all the people they are walking around
One being peaceful or horrid or lonely or bored
Or pleasant and contented the right kind
Of civilization could be good for all these people
And certainly food would be good for the hungry people
And limitations must be placed on the greedy people
And guns must be taken away from the aggressive people
And medicine must be given to the ailing people
And so on and each individual one of the people
Who dreams every night (it is supposed) may be supposed
To have the seething and the golden curiosity. How to organize the
    thing
So that each of these people
Is happy with it, happy with him, with her, and me
And we also are, and it, and all, with them? That would be the day—
How can it be with everyone feeling he is the main one and the germs
    there every day?

8

Different civilizations simultaneously existing,
Indian in the throes of one, samurai in the waning of another,
Heck-saying businessman in mine, and little civilizations suggesting
    something
Like farmyard civilization, fishingman and net and boat civilization,
And then back to your own and to my own, all the
Efficiency the good will the weakness and the snobbery
The uncertainty the recovery the rather long life the bursts
Of helpless enthusiasm the sweet reformers in the streets
Today as I just looked out the window and here come the riot police
And the sitting inside and not knowing if I should be outside, in the
    midst of this.
The orchestra plays and everyone is growing up and being
One of who are a various number of beings

Simultaneously dreaming of existing
As the civilizations say they are when we speak.

9

To be a back, which doesn't break, and to hate what is mysterious
That doesn't need to be, grant me O Athena
Of the roses and the gamma globulin—however, prayer
Is nothing I can ever be serious about (I think).
The answer is elusive and the work about it goes on
A long time and so we want our lives to go on
Among other things in hope to find an answer. Though we know
That the answer of eighty will not be the answer of eighteen.
En route we give titles to things, we further
Complicate our own situation and that of other persons
And we get wiser, sometimes, and kinder, and probably less exciting
(Certainly so), and grow out of our illusions (sometimes) and so
Can look around and say, Oh! So! but usually without the time
Or power to change anything (sometimes—maybe a fraction—if so, it's
    amazing!)—then off we go.

Fate

In a room on West Tenth Street in June
Of nineteen fifty-one, Frank O'Hara and I
And Larry Rivers (I actually do not remember
If Larry was there, but he would be there
Later, some winter night, on the stairway
Sitting waiting, "a demented telephone"
As Frank said in an article about him but then
On the stairs unhappy in a youthful manner, much
Happened later), Frank, John Ashbery,
Jane Freilicher and I, and I
Had just come back from Europe for the first time.
I had a bottle of Irish whiskey I had
Bought in Shannon, where the plane stopped
And we drank it and I told
My friends about Europe, they'd never
Been there, how much I'd loved it, I
Was so happy to be there with them, and my
Europe, too, which I had, Greece, Italy, France,
Scandinavia, and England—imagine
Having all that the first time. The walls
Were white in that little apartment, so tiny
The rooms are so small but we all fitted into one
And talked, Frank so sure of his
Talent but didn't say it that way, I
Didn't know it till after he was
Dead just how sure he had been, and John
Unhappy and brilliant and silly and of them all my
First friend, we had met at Harvard they
Tended except Frank to pooh-pooh
What I said about Europe and even
Frank was more interested but ever polite
When sober I couldn't tell it but
Barely tended they tended to be much more
Interested in gossip such as
Who had been sleeping with whom and what
Was selling and going on whereat I
Was a little hurt but used to it my

Expectations from my friendships were
Absurd but that way I got so
Much out of them in fact it wasn't
Causal but the two ways at once I was
Never so happy with anyone
As I was with those friends
At that particular time on that day with
That bottle of Irish whiskey the time
Four in the afternoon or
Three in the afternoon or two or five
I don't know what and why do I think
That my being so happy is so urgent
And important? it seems some kind
Of evidence of the truth as if
I could go back and take it? or do
I just want to hold what
There is of it now? thinking says hold
Something now which is why
Despite me and liking me that
Afternoon who was sleeping with
Whom was best and
My happiness picking up
A glass Frank What was it like Kenny
Ah from my being vulnerable
Only sometimes I can see the vulnerable-
Ness in others I have ever known
Faults with them or on the telephone
The sexual adventures were different
Each person at work autobiography all
The time plowing forward if
There's no question of movement as there
Isn't no doubt of it may I not
I may find this moment minute
Extraordinary? I can do nothing
With it but write about it two
Hundred forty West
Tenth Street, Jane's apartment,

Nineteen fifty-one or fifty-two I
Can never remember yes it was
Later or much earlier
That Larry sat on the stairs
And John said Um hum and hum and hum I
Don't remember the words Frank said Un hun
Jane said An Han and Larry if he
Was there said Boobledyboop so always
Said Larry or almost and I said
Aix-en-Provence me new sense of
These that London Firenze Florence
Now Greece and un hun um hum an
Han boop Soon I was at Larry's
And he's proposing we take a
House in Eastham—what? for the
Summer where is that and
Already that afternoon was dissipated
Another begun many more of
Them but that was one
I remember I was in
A special position as if it
Were my birthday but
They were in fact as if my
Birthday or that is to say Who
Cares if he grows older if
He has friends like
These I mean who does not
Care? the celebration is the cause
Of the sorrow and not
The other way around. I also went
To Venice and to Vienna there were
Some people I drove there
With new sunshine Frank says
Let's go out Jane John Frank
And I (Larry was not there, I now
Remember) then mysteriously
Left

The Simplicity of the Unknown Past

Out the window, the cow out the window
The steel frame out the window, the rusted candlestand;
Out the window the horse, the handle-less pan,
Real things. Inside the window my heart
That only beats for you—a verse of Verlaine.
Inside the window of my heart is a style
And a showplace of onion-like construction.
Inside the window is a picture of a cat
And outside the window is the cat indeed
Jumping up now to the top of the
Roof of the garage; its paws help take it there.
Inside this window is a range
Of things which outside the window are like stars
Arranged but huge in fashion.
Outside the window is a car, is the rusted wheel of a bicycle.
Inside it are words and paints; outside, smooth hair
Of a rabbit, just barely seen. Inside the glass
Of this window is a notebook, with little marks,
They are words. Outside this window is a wall
With little parts—they are stones. Inside this window
Is the start, and outside is the beginning. A heart
Beats. The cat leaps. The room is light, the sun is almost blinding.
Inside this body is a woman, inside whom is a star
Of some kind or other, which is like a uterus; and
Outside the window a farm machine starts.

The Burning Mystery of Anna in 1951

I. THE BURNING MYSTERY OF ANNA

"I don't know how to kiss."
Won't you come in?

To have bent her back half across the bed.
To be so bending her.

Not yet having said Won't you come in.
Never yet having said it.

Planning to say, Can we
Would you like to come up to my room?

The bedroom stairway
And then thought about it.

My name is you.
I am not interested him the first place.

I come from Corsica.
The scene is very confusing.

She is dancing and I
Think she is pretty. That's one part of it.

2. WHY NOT?

It is satisfying to have a nose
Right in the middle of my face.

You asked me the question and I replied
With as much imagination as I could.

Then one foggy morning we met.
We sat in a cold café and compared viruses.

Oh, sure, I'd heard of you a thousand times
From E and L and X and A and Y.

What was I trying to hide? Something monstrous?
Is there really anything to hide?

I hate all these guiltmongers. God damn it,
I said to myself one day. I'll let fly!

The story of my existence as I reconstruct it
Now is about one sixth part reconstruction.

Suggested to me by plastic instead of cork
In the bottleneck I said, Well listen, now, well, well, to hell with it!
    Why not?

3. WITH DAD

The fly I cast was red.
Dad said Push it!

We went out in the boat.
Marble-like was the sea.

Down to the sand we went
And to the dock next.

Let's go fishing said Dad.
I pulled on red sweater.

I was sitting on the porch
Peacefully when Dad marched out.

This is one of my experiences
Which I think is fairly typical.

You've asked me to tell you
A little bit about my life.

Hello. How are you? I'm fine,
Thanks. Today there is something new.

4. STARTING

The oranges subdued the attack
Or rather we endured it.

I am tired of being attacked, she said.
Then the rain fell.

It was a sunny morning.
Sunny sunny sunny sunny sunny.

The night was dark. The dogs
Howled till it got sunny.

The young man is living with the French
Family near the entrance to the trough.

Actual cash value nineteen dollars.
He puts it on but then she takes it off.

What was it I remembered of L. at school?
A keen bursitis lit the window.

Simple simple simple, simply to start,
To be so easy when one is at the start.

5. A CRITICAL POINT

She: Weren't you curious about our conversation?
I said: I have been watching you all from here.

Then I went up to her and started to speak.
I felt shy but I had to confront the beautiful.

Talking to another stranger, I think a guy
In the distance I saw her, the checked-print-dressed girl I had seen.

Wandering along through the twisting streets of the city
One day as I was, as is my habit.

Perfectly true, but on this day it was different.
You always do the same things every day.

Get up, brush your teeth, eat breakfast, then wander.
I really don't see how you can stand the boredom.

I hope you don't mind if I'm a little critical
I'm afraid that you won't like what I'm going to say.

I had something to say she had never heard.
A bird woke me this morning with the usual.

6. TWO BICYCLE RIDERS

It is the summer of genius! And also of genes!
You replied, as I gulped over the hill-Alps.

What is the nature of things, I replied,
As we tortured the hill-Alps.

179

This answers all questions, you described,
As we biked over the hill-Alps.

Then tell me more, I think I squeaked,
As we broke the chains of the hill-Alps.

And so that's the truth, you indicted,
As we tore down the mounts of the hill-Alps.

The mention is cotton to the street
Which in turn encapsules drifted attention.

Finally, with courage mounting, I asked you,
What are we doing on these hill-Alps?

O beautiful person silent and serene
Invited by me to pedal on these mountains.

7. ABSTRACT

Unavoidable and inescapable.
What is your nature? I said.

Quiet, but how to make them,
Also, grabbing of the spirit?

Admirable, I said.
They presented a problem.

When I first saw them
They felt complete.

Come, said my mind,
I will show them to you.

Where are these new
Unities? I said.

Then something rainbowed
And a new thing promised.

I was living. I said,
I can do all that I wish.

8. WHAT I WAS THINKING OF

The reeds were very sunny. "Yes, he
Lived here—Cézanne," you said.

Retiring from the bicycles and remarking
How painful it was to bike, pleasanter to walk.

Was it the day a man with a moustache, a girl
Anne, three law students and I went?

Come on, let's go for a walk!
Bring not the bicycle.

Je crois qu'il éxagère, says Marguérite.
Then, twoo-twoo, outside hear a bell.

Up to lunch from the wall about which I wrote
The poem "Bricks."

Standing in the sunlight and thinking
Or doing something like that.

First getting up and down the hill
Walking, until I smelled the fields, on two legs.

In the Morning

In the morning the only thing moving was the garbage on the water.
In the afternoon the fellaheen stormed their tents.
We bought cold cream and lay in the sun.

The birches against the risotto are climbing the arches.
Ah, well, it's a young tree's privilege to climb.
These older torches are scaling the flagons of the night.

Going to parties often meant a welcome
To some new, dear, or old and trusted friend.
Often it meant the chance to make new friendships somewhat in transit.

He felt the new collars and the catalogues
Of old dresses. I'll take this one and this one, said he.
Meanwhile a dark red velvet was staring him in the face.

Baron Haussmann, Claude Debussy, and Sherwood Anderson . . .
Time to get up and go out and feel one's new collar
And the elevator's fresh young smell in the quiet building.

The rats fell, one by one, from the Pontiff's apartment.
It had no political significance. The building was being cleaned.
Music blared, and some of the faithful were touched on the shoulder by
    rats.

We move into the apartments of day. They fold and enwrap us.
The steam rises from their edges. Rat runs past.
Pink clouds of dust jump up. He feels the collar—it's a little cold.

There isn't anything there except what's real.
He walks out feeling his nape. This is sunny weather.
Suddenly the elevator rises to the floor above.

George Bernard Shaw, the Empress of Roumania, Immanuel Kant . . .
He pokes the trees. It's a pleasure to show you these ruins.
This invitation admits one. My son is sleeping.

He wanders in the sense of having only one place to go.
The elevator ambiance is waiting.
Orchids, Impressionism, ice machines, daggers, and bends.

Forms have an attraction to which we gradually yield.
Josephine Baker, Respighi, La Contessa di Alba.
He believed that the city was steel, but it was only the sun. I want to
    see you.

Come over for breakfast. A cow eats a grassblade. Containers.
Our babies will need plenty of milk. He says, I am leaving Paris.
Sohrab and Rustum, Childe Harold's Pilgrimage, the Dybbuk, Titian's
    Assumption.

A swirl of red robes at the throat. Goodbye . . . Are—? Speechless.
The asterisks dust on the paper. Will I see you again?
Boris Pasternak, Abraham Lincoln, Socrates, Orion . . .

I've wanted to ask you one question. She has a baby.
Room full of stars and iridium, eyelids which dazzle.
What can a life be without you? The words didn't say.

I don't want you to be so serious . . .
When he got back, she was already at the door.
Eleanora Duse, Emily Dickinson, Job, Karl Marx, Atalanta. . . .

The Boiling Water

A serious moment for the water is when it boils
And though one usually regards it merely as a convenience
To have the boiling water available for bath or table
Occasionally there is someone around who understands
The importance of this moment for the water—maybe a saint,
Maybe a poet, maybe a crazy man, or just someone temporarily
    disturbed
With his mind "floating," in a sense, away from his deepest
Personal concerns to more "unreal" things. A lot of poetry
Can come from perceptions of this kind, as well as a lot of insane
    conversations.
Intense people can sometimes get stuck on topics like these
And keep you far into the night with them. Still, it is true
That the water has just started to boil. How important
For the water! And now I see that the tree is waving in the wind
(I assume it is the wind)—at least, its branches are. In order to see
Hidden meanings, one may have to ignore
The most exciting ones, those that are most directly appealing
And yet it is only these appealing ones that, often, one can trust
To make one's art solid and true, just as it is sexual attraction
One has to trust, often, in love. So the boiling water's seriousness
Is likely to go unobserved until the exact strange moment
(And what a temptation it is to end the poem here
With some secret thrust) when it involuntarily comes into the mind
And then one can write of it. A serious moment for this poem will be
    when it ends,
It will be like the water's boiling, that for which we've waited
Without trying to think of it too much, since "a watched pot never
    boils,"
And a poem with its ending figured out is difficult to write.

Once the water is boiling, the heater has a choice: to look at it
And let it boil and go on seeing what it does, or to take it off and use
    the water for tea,
Chocolate, or coffee, or beef consommé. You don't drink the product
    then
Until the water has ceased to boil, for otherwise

It would burn your tongue. Even hot water is dangerous and has a
thorn
Like the rose, or a horn like the baby ram. Modest hot water, and the
tree
Blowing in the wind. The connection here is how serious is it for the
tree
To have its arms wave (its branches)? How did it ever get such
flexibility
In the first place? and who put the boiling potentiality into water?
A tree will not boil, nor will the wind. Think of the dinners
We could have, and the dreams, if only they did.
But that is not to think of what things are really about. For the tree
I don't know how serious it is to be waving, though water's boiling
Is more dramatic, is more like a storm, high tide
And the ship goes down, but it comes back up as coffee, chocolate, or
tea.

How many people I have drunk tea or coffee with
And thought about the boiling water hardly at all, just waiting for it to
boil
So there could be coffee or chocolate or tea. And then what?
The body stimulated, the brain alarmed, grounds in the pot,
The tree, waving, out the window, perhaps with a little more élan
Because we saw it that way, because the water boiled, because we drank
tea.

The water boils almost every time the same old way
And still it is serious, because it is boiling. That is what,
I think, one should see. From this may come compassion,
Compassion and a knowledge of nature, although most of the time
I know I am not going to think about it. It would be crazy
To give such things precedence over such affairs of one's life
As involve more fundamental satisfactions. But is going to the beach
More fundamental than seeing the water boil? Saving of money,
It's well known, can result from an aesthetic attitude, since a rock
Picked up in the street contains all the shape and hardness of the world.
One sidewalk leads everywhere. You don't have to be in Estapan.

A serious moment for the island is when its trees
Begin to give it shade, and another is when the ocean washes
Big heavy things against its side. One walks around and looks at the
    island
But not really at it, at what is on it, and one thinks,
It must be serious, even, to be this island, at all, here,
Since it is lying here exposed to the whole sea. All its
Moments might be serious. It is serious, in such windy weather, to be a
    sail
Or an open window, or a feather flying in the street.

Seriousness, how often I have thought of seriousness
And how little I have understood it, except this: serious is urgent
And it has to do with change. You say to the water,
It's not necessary to boil now, and you turn it off. It stops
Fidgeting. And starts to cool. You put your hand in it
And say, The water isn't serious any more. It has the potential,
However—that urgency to give off bubbles, to
Change itself to steam. And the wind,
When it becomes part of a hurricane, blowing up the beach
And the sand dunes can't keep it away.
Fainting is one sign of seriousness, crying is another.
Shuddering all over is another one.

A serious moment for the telephone is when it rings,
And a person answers, it is Angelica, or is it you
And finally, at last, who answer, my wing, my past, my
Angel, my flume, and my de-control, my orange and my good-bye kiss,
My extravagance, and my weight at fifteen years old
And at the height of my intelligence, oh Cordillera two
And sandals one, C'est toi à l'appareil? Is that you at
The telephone, and when it snows, a serious moment for the bus is when
    it snows
For then it has to slow down for sliding, and every moment is a trust.

A serious moment for the fly is when its wings
Are moving, and a serious moment for the duck

Is when it swims, when it first touches water, then spreads
Its smile upon the water, its feet begin to paddle, it is in
And above the water, pushing itself forward, a duck.
And a serious moment for the sky is when, completely blue,
It feels some clouds coming; another when it turns dark.
A serious moment for the match is when it bursts into flame
And is all alone, living, in that instant, that beautiful second for which it
   was made.
So much went into it! The men at the match factory, the mood of
The public, the sand covering the barn
So it was hard to find the phosphorus, and now this flame,
This pink white ecstatic light blue! For the telephone when it rings,
For the wind when it blows, and for the match when it bursts into
   flame.

Serious, all our life is serious, and we see around us
Seriousness for other things, that touches us and seems as if it might be
   giving clues.
The seriousness of the house when it is being built
And is almost completed, and then the moment when it is completed.
The seriousness of the bee when it stings. We say, He has taken his life,
Merely to sting. Why would he do that? And we feel
We aren't concentrated enough, not pure, not deep
As the buzzing bee. The bee flies into the house
And lights on a chair arm and sits there, waiting for something to be
Other than it is, so he can fly again. He is boiling, waiting. Soon he is
   forgotten
And everyone is speaking again.

Seriousness, everyone speaks of seriousness
Certain he knows or seeking to know what it is. A child is bitten by an
   animal
And that is serious. The doctor has a serious life. He is somewhat, in
   that, like the bee.
And water! water—how it is needed! and it is always going down
Seeking its own level, evaporating, boiling, now changing into ice
And snow, now making up our bodies. We drink the coffee

And somewhere in this moment is the chance
We will never see each other again. It is serious for the tree
To be moving, the flexibility of its moving
Being the sign of its continuing life. And now there are its blossoms
And the fact that it is blossoming again, it is filling up with
Pink and whitish blossoms, it is full of them, the wind blows, it is
Warm, though, so much is happening, it is spring, the people step out
And doors swing in, and billions of insects are born. You call me and
    tell me
You feel your life isn't worth living. I say that I'm coming to see you. I
    put the key in
And the car begins to clatter, and now it starts.

Serious for me that I met you, and serious for you
That you met me, and that we do not know
If we will ever be close to anyone again. Serious the recognition of the
    probability
That we will, although time stretches terribly in between. It is serious
    not to know
And to know and to try to figure things out. One's legs
Cross, foot swings, and a cigarette is blooming, a gray bouquet, and
The water is boiling. Serious the birth (what a phenomenon!) of
    anything and
The movements of the trees, and for the lovers
Everything they do and see. Serious intermittently for consciousness
The sign that something may be happening, always, today,
That is enough. For the germ when it enters or leaves a body. For the
    fly when it lifts its little wings.

To Marina

So many convolutions and not enough simplicity!
When I had you to write to it
Was different. The quiet, dry Z
Leaped up to the front of the alphabet.
You sit, stilling your spoons
With one hand; you move them with the other.
Radio says, "God is a postmaster."
You said, Ziss is lawflee. And in the heat
Of writing to you I wrote simply. I thought
These are the best things I shall ever write
And have ever written. I thought of nothing but touching you.
Thought of seeing you and, in a separate thought, of looking at you.
You were concentrated feeling and thought.
You were like the ocean
In which my poems were the swimming. I brought you
Earrings. You said, These are lawflee. We went
To some beach, where the sand was dirty. Just going in
To the bathing house with you drove me "out of my mind."

It is wise to be witty. The shirt collar's far away.
Men tramp up and down the city on this windy day.
I am feeling a-political as a shell
Brought off some fish. Twenty-one years
Ago I saw you and loved you still.
Still! It wasn't plenty
Of time. Read Anatole France. Bored, a little. Read
Tolstoy, replaced and overcome. You read Stendhal.
I told you to. Where was replacement
Then? I don't know. He shushed us back into ourselves.
I used to understand
The highest excitement. Someone died
And you were distant. I went away
And made you distant. Where are you now? I see the chair
And hang onto it for sustenance. Good God how you kissed me
And I held you. You screamed
And I wasn't bothered by anything. Was nearest you.

And you were so realistic
Preferring the Soviet Bookstore
To my literary dreams.
"You don't like war," you said
After reading a poem
In which I'd simply said I hated war
In a whole list of things. To you
It seemed a position, to me
It was all a flux, especially then.
I was in an
Unexpected situation.
Let's take a walk
I wrote. And I love you as a sheriff
Searches for a walnut. And And so unless
I'm going to see your face
Bien soon, and you said
You must take me away, and
Oh Kenneth
You like everything
To be pleasant. I was burning
Like an arch
Made out of trees.

I'm not sure we ever actually took a walk.
We were so damned nervous. I was heading somewhere. And you had to
    be
At an appointment, or else be found out! Illicit love!
It's not a thing to think of. Nor is it when it's licit!
It is too much! And it wasn't enough. The achievement
I thought I saw possible when I loved you
Was that really achievement? Were you my
Last chance to feel that I had lost my chance?
I grew faint at your voice on the telephone
Electricity and all colors were mine, and the tops of hills
And everything that breathes. That was a feeling. Certain
Artistic careers had not even started. And I
Could have surpassed them. I could have I think put the

Whole world under our feet. You were in the restaurant. It
Was Chinese. We have walked three blocks. Or four blocks. It is New
York
In nineteen fifty-three. Nothing has as yet happened
That will ever happen and will mean as much to me. You smile, and
turn your head.

What rocketing there was in my face and in my head
And bombing everywhere in my body
I loved you I knew suddenly
That nothing had meant anything like you
I must have hoped (crazily) that something would
As if thinking you were the person I had become.

My sleep is beginning to be begun. And the sheets were on the bed.
A clock rang a bird's song rattled into my typewriter.
I had been thinking about songs which were very abstract.
Language was the champion. The papers lay piled on my desk
It was really a table. Now, the telephone. Hello, what?
What is my life like now? Engaged, studying and looking around
The library, teaching—I took it rather easy
A little too easy—we went to the ballet
Then dark becomes the light (blinding) of the next eighty days.
Orchestra cup became As beautiful as an orchestra or a cup, and
Locked climbs becomes If we were locked, well not quite, rather
Oh penniless could I really die, and I understood everything
Which before was running this way and that in my head
I saw titles, volumes, and suns I felt the hot
Pressure of your hands in that restaurant
To which, along with glasses, plates, lamps, lusters,
Tablecloths, napkins, and all the other junk
You added my life for it was entirely in your hands then—
My life
Yours, My Sister Life of Pasternak's beautiful title
My life without a life, my life in a life, my life impure
And my life pure, life seen as an entity

One death and a variety of days
And only one life.

I wasn't ready
For you.

I understood nothing
Seemingly except my feelings
You were whirling
In your life
I was keeping
Everything in my head
An artist friend's apartment
Five flights up the
Lower East Side nineteen
Fifty-something I don't know
What we made love the first time I
Almost died I had never felt
That way it was like being stamped on in Hell
It was roses of Heaven
My friends seemed turned to me to empty shell

On the railroad train's red velvet back
You put your hand in mine and said
"I told him"
Or was it the time after that?
I said Why did you
Do that you said I thought
It was over. Why? Because you were so
Nervous of my being there it was something I thought

I read
Tolstoy. You said
I don't like the way it turns out (*Anna
Karenina*) I had just liked the strength
Of the feeling you thought
About the end. I wanted
To I don't know what never leave you

Five flights up the June
Street emptied of fans, cups, kites, cops, eats, nights, no
The night was there
And something like air I love you Marina
Eighty-five days
Four thousand three hundred and sixty-
Two minutes all poetry was changed
For me what did I do in exchange
I am selfish, afraid you are
Overwhelmingly parade, back, sunshine, dreams
Later thousands of dreams

You said
You make me feel nawble (noble). I said
Yes. I said
To nothingness, This is all poems. Another one said (later)
That is so American. You were Russian.
You thought of your feelings, one said, not of her,
Not of the real situation. But my feelings were a part,
They were the force of the real situation. Truer to say I thought
Not of the whole situation
For your husband was also a part
And your feelings about your child were a part
And all my other feelings were a part. We
Turned this way and that, up-
Stairs then down
Into the streets.
Did I die because I didn't stay with you?
Or what did I lose of my life? I lost
You. I put you
In everything I wrote.

I used that precious material I put it in forms
Also I wanted to break down the forms
Poetry was a real occupation
To hell with the norms, with what is already written
Twenty-nine in love finds pure expression

Twenty-nine years you my whole life's digression
Not taken and Oh Kenneth
Everything afterwards seemed nowhere near
What I could do then in several minutes—
I wrote,
"I want to look at you all day long
Because you are mine."

I am twenty-nine, pocket flap folded
And I am smiling I am looking out at a world that
I significantly re-created from inside
Out of contradictory actions and emotions. I look like a silly child that
Photograph that year—big glasses, unthought-of clothes,
A suit, slight mess in general, cropped hair. And someone liked me,
Loved me a lot, I think. And someone else had, you had, too. I was
Undrenched by the tears I'd shed later about this whole thing when
I'd telephone you I'd be all nerves, though in fact
All life was a factor and all my nerves were in my head. I feel
Peculiar. Or I feel nothing. I am thinking about this poem. I am
    thinking about your raincoat,
I am worried about the tactfulness,
About the truth of what I say.
I am thinking about my standards for my actions
About what they were
You raised my standards for harmony and for happiness so much
And, too, the sense of a center
Which did amazing things for my taste
But my taste for action? for honesty, for directness in behavior?
I believe I simply never felt that anything could go wrong
This was abject stupidity
I also was careless in how I drove then and in what I ate
And drank it was easier to feel that nothing could go wrong
I had those feelings. I
Did not those things. I was involved in such and such
A situation, artistically and socially. We never spent a night
Together it is the New York of

Aquamarine sunshine and the Loew's Theater's blazing swing of light
In the middle of the day

Let's take a walk
Into the world
Where if our shoes get white
With snow, is it snow, Marina,
Is it snow or light?
Let's take a walk

Every detail is everything in its place (Aristotle). Literature is a cup
And we are the malted. The time is a glass. A June bug comes
And a carpenter spits on a plane, the flowers ruffle ear rings.
I am so dumb-looking. And you are so beautiful.

Sitting in the Hudson Tube
Walking up the fusky street
Always waiting to see you
You the original creation of all my You, you the you
In every poem the hidden one whom I am talking to
Worked at Bamberger's once I went with you to Cerutti's
Bar—on Madison Avenue? I held your hand and you said
Kenneth you are playing with fire. I said
Something witty in reply.
It was the time of the McCarthy trial
Hot sunlight on lunches. You squirted
Red wine into my mouth.
My feelings were like a fire my words became very clear
My psyche or whatever it is that puts together motions and emotions
Was unprepared. There was a good part
And an alarmingly bad part which didn't correspond—
No letters! no seeming connection! your slim pale hand
It actually was, your blondness and your turning-around-to-me look.
    Good-bye Kenneth.

No, Marina, don't go
And what had been before would come after

Not to be mysterious we'd be together make love again
It was the wildest thing I've done
I can hardly remember it
It has gotten by now
So mixed up with losing you
The two almost seem in some way the same. You
Wore something soft—angora? cashmere?
I remember that it was black. You turned around
And on such a spring day which went on and on and on
I actually think I felt that I could keep
The strongest of all feelings contained inside me
Producing endless emotional designs.

With the incomparable feeling of rising and of being like a banner
Twenty seconds worth twenty-five years
With feeling noble extremely mobile and very free
With Taking a Walk With You, West Wind, In Love With You, and
    Yellow Roses
With pleasure I felt my leg muscles and my brain couldn't hold
With the Empire State Building the restaurant your wrist bones with
    Greenwich Avenue
In nineteen fifty-one with heat humidity a dog pissing with neon
With the feeling that at last
My body had something to do and so did my mind

You sit
At the window. You call
Me, across Paris,
Amsterdam, New
York. Kenneth!
My Soviet
Girlhood. My
Spring, summer
And fall. Do you
Know you have
Missed some of them?
Almost all. I am

Waiting and I
Am fading I
Am fainting I'm
In a degrading state
Of inactivity. A ball
Rolls in the gutter. I have
Two hands to
Stop it. I am
A flower I pick
The vendor his
Clothes getting up
Too early and
What is it makes this rose
Into what is more fragrant than what is not?

I am stunned I am feeling tortured
By "A man of words and not a man of deeds"

I was waiting in a taxicab
It was white letters in white paints it was you
Spring comes, summer, then fall
And winter. We really have missed
All of that, whatever else there was
In those years so sanded by our absence.
I never saw you for as long as half a day.

You were crying outside the bus station
And I was crying—
I knew that this really was my life—
I kept thinking of how we were crying
Later, when I was speaking, driving, walking,
Looking at doorways and colors, mysterious entrances
Sometimes I'd be pierced as by a needle
Sometimes be feverish as from a word
Books closed and I'd think
I can't read this book, I threw away my life
These held on to their lives. I was

Excited by praise from anyone, startled by criticism, always hating it
Traveling around Europe and being excited
It was all in reference to you
And feeling I was not gradually forgetting
What your temples and cheekbones looked like
And always with this secret.

Later I thought
That what I had done was reasonable
It may have been reasonable
I also thought that I saw what had appealed to me
So much about you, the way you responded
To everything your excitement about
Me, I had never seen that. And the fact
That you were Russian, very mysterious, all that I didn't know
About you—and you didn't know
Me, for I was as strange to you as you were to me.
You were like my first trip to France you had
Made no assumptions. I could be
Clearly and passionately and
Nobly (as you'd said) who I was—at the outer limits of my life
Of my life as my life could be
Ideally. But what about the dark part all this lifted
Me out of? Would my bad moods, my uncertainties, my
Distrust of people I was close to, the
Twisty parts of my ambition, my
Envy, all have gone away? And if
They hadn't gone, what? For didn't I need
All the strength you made me feel I had, to deal
With the difficulties of really having you?
Where could we have been? But I saw so many new possibilities
That it made me rather hate reality
Or I think perhaps I already did
I didn't care about the consequences
Because they weren't "poetic" weren't "ideal"

And oh well you said we walk along
Your white dress your blue dress your green
Blouse with sleeves then one without
Sleeves and we are speaking
Of things but not of very much because underneath it
I am raving I am boiling I am afraid
You ask me Kenneth what are you thinking
If I could say
It all then I thought if I could say
Exactly everything and have it still be as beautiful
Billowing over, riding over both our doubts
Some kind of perfection and what did I actually
Say? Marina it's late. Marina
It's early. I love you. Or else, What's this street?
You were the perfection of my life
And I couldn't have you. That is, I didn't.
I couldn't think. I wrote, instead. I would have had
To think hard, to figure everything out
About how I could be with you,
Really, which I couldn't do
In those moments of permanence we had
As we walked along.

We walk through the park in the sun. It is the end.
You phone me. I send you a telegram. It
Is the end. I keep
Thinking about you, grieving about you. It is the end. I write
Poems about you, to you. They
Are no longer simple. No longer
Are you there to see every day or
Every other or every third or fourth warm day
And now it has been twenty-five years
But those feelings kept orchestrating I mean rehearsing
Rehearsing in me and tuning up
While I was doing a thousand other things, the band
Is ready, I am over fifty years old and there's no you—
And no me, either, not as I was then,

When it was the Renaissance
Filtered through my nerves and weakness
Of nineteen fifty-four or fifty-three,
When I had you to write to, when I could see you
And it could change.

from

Days
and
Nights

In Bed

MORNINGS IN BED

Are energetic mornings.

SNOW IN BED

When we got out of bed
It was snowing.

MEN IN BED

All over Paris
Men are in bed.

BEAUTIFUL GIRL IN BED

Why I am happy to be here.

LONG RELATIONSHIP IN BED

The springs and the bedposts
Are ready the minute we come in.

DOLLS IN BED

With little girls.

HAMMER AND NAILS IN BED

To make it better
They are making it a better bed
And a bigger bed, firmer and larger
And finer bed. So the hammer and nails in the bed
And the carpenter's finger
And thumb and his eyes and his shoulder.
Bang! Bang! Smap! The hammer and nails in bed.

SHEEP IN BED

The sheep got into the bed
By mistake.

BUYING A NEW BED

One of the first things you did
Was buy a new bed.

WINDOW IN BED

I looked at you
And you looked back.

MARRIED IN BED

We'll be married in bed.
The preachers, the witnesses, and all our families
Will also be in bed.

POETRY BED

Whenas in bed
Then, then

OTHER POETRY BED

Shall I compare you to a summer's bed?
You are more beautiful.

ORCHIDS IN BED

She placed orchids in the bed
On that dark blue winter morning.

LYING IN BED

Bed with Spain in it
Bed with Gibraltar in it
Bed of art!

LOVERS IN BED

Are lovers no more
Than lovers on the street.

(See Picasso's "Pair of Young Mountebanks," FC 533,
Greuze's "Noces," or hear Mozart's "Fleichtscausenmusik," Köchel 427)

SOME BED

Once
Held
This
All

GOD IN BED

Christ
Was not
Born
(And did
Not die)
In a bed.

LÉGER IN BED

Above our apartment
In 1955
Lived Fernand Léger.

SHOUTING IN BED

We wake up
To the sound of shouts.

FRIENDS IN BED

Sleep well.

ANGELIC CEREMONY IN BED

Putting on the sheets.

MYSTERY OF BED

She takes it for granted
That he will stay up all night long.

WORKMEN IN BED

With workmen's wives
And workmen's girl friends
And other workmen
And dolls.

ACAPULCO IN BED

In Mexico, with blue shimmering water,
Acapulco is in bed.

MY INTOXICATION IN BED

Was not long-lasting.
Was fantastic.
Did not lead me to be very well-mannered.
Wasn't completely romantic.

BASKETBALL IN BED

The basketball is thrown on the bed.

EXPENSIVE BED

At the Lutétia 500 francs a night
In the Hôpital St-Antoine 1000 francs a night

THEATRICAL BED

Exceeded expectations
And received applause.

SIRENS IN BED

My face is plastered to the window
When the sirens come.

COURTSHIP IN BED

"Please. Tell me you like me."
"How did you get in this bed?"

WET DOG IN BED

There is nothing like a wet dog in bed.

DOG BED

In the dog bed
I cannot sleep.

ATOMIC BED

Billions of—uncountable—electrons
Compose this bed.

BEING IN BED

Belongs to everyone
Bed with Spain in it
Bed of art!

SNOW IN BED (LATER)

When it stopped snowing
We still hadn't gone to bed

PHILOSOPHY IN BED

(I)
Plato says this bed
Isn't the real one.
What did Plato know
About beds?

(II)
Spinoza constructed a bed
Which was slept in by Alfred North Whitehead.

(XLIV)
You say, "Let's go to bed"
But those words have no meaning.

SOUTH AMERICA IN BED

Brazil, Argentina, Ecuador, and Peru
Are in bed. The first thing you did
Was to buy a new bed.

AS WE LAY IN BED

We saw the stars starting to come together
As we lay in bed.

POLIZIANO IN BED

Angelo Poliziano
Never went to bed
Was it he or Castiglione—
The perfect Renaissance man?

LUNCH IN BED

It's late! Get up! The roseate fruit trees
Are blushing with the nape of new-frocked day!
Awake! The modern breeze of spring
Is pulsative through nest-caroming branches!

COWARDS IN BED

Afraid to turn over. Come on. Come on, turn over. Cowards in bed.

CHOPIN'S ÉTUDES IN BED

Here is the bed
Of Chopin's Études;
Over here is his Préludes' bed;
And here is the bed of his Mazurkas.

PRÉLUDES IN BED

There are no préludes in bed
Today.

LET'S GO TO BED

When the tree
Is blossoming. It will be
A long time
Before it is blossoming again.

STONES IN BED

In the bed are stones
From Egypt and Etruria
And some magazines and a pouch of tobacco.

BED

I'd wake up every morning
And look out the window across the park.

WOODEN MECHANICAL FIGURE INDICATING A BED

With a mighty smile
And a mighty gesture
He discloses the bed.

Y. SICK IN BED

Said, If there is a heaven
I want it to look
Like what is out there.

MORNINGS IN BED

Are pensive mornings.

SUICIDE

I was unable to tell you any reason
To get out of bed

209

A BLUE AND WHITE BED

Became a yellow and gold one,
Then was green, pale green,
Then violet, then onyx,
Yes onyx, then it was an onyx bed.

BALCONIES IN BED

When you lean over
When you fall
When you speak

BEDS IN THE GARDENS OF SPAIN

To the sound of a guitar
When you enter the room.

POETRY IN BED

Do you remember how this started—
With "Mornings in Bed" and "Snow in Bed"?

RISPETTO

Good-bye to bed.
The ceiling loses its chance
To see you smile again
In just that way.

LUXEMBOURG BED

The bed flies past
Like a swing.

ADVANCE BED

Advance arm. Advance stairs. Advance power.
Advance bed.

CHILD BED

You had two babies
Before we met

ABSTRACT BED

There is paint
On the abstract bed.

ORCHIDS IN BED

She placed orchids on the bed
On a dark red winter afternoon.

AT ENDEBED

At Endebed I mett you
You go up on the lift, no, yes
Then we hearing from sounds of guitars
Americans strolling bingo hatrack in the lake.

ENEMIES IN BED

Enemies sleep in separate beds
But in the same part of the city.

PRIMAVERA

He makes up the bed
And follows her home.

ESTATE

The bed lies in the room
The way she lies in the bed.

SAWBED

In the bed of the saw
The sawdust is dying.

WINDOWBED

From henna to blue all violet is in bed.

ZEN BED

I can't get to bed.
Show me the bed and I will show you how to get to it.

LARGE SUNDAY BED

Domingo.
Domenica.
Dimanche.

SATURDAY BED

Sabato.

SNOW IN BED

When we get out of bed
There is no more bed.

WOMEN IN BED

Everywhere in Paris
Women are in bed.

MARRIED IN BED

We did not get married
In bed.

FALSE BED

There are Easter eggs
Red blue yellow and white-pink
In the false bed.

INVITING SOMEONE FROM BED

Come, let me help you out of bed.
The sun is shining. The window is open. Look!
From the balcony there is the street, which is like a bed.

THE FUTURE BED

Will be lilac in color
And in the shape of an L or a Z.

GUITARS IN BED

When we get out of bed
We hear guitars.

POST-MODERNISM IN BED

Kandinsky, Arp, Valéry, Léger, and Marinetti
Are kicked out of bed.
Then, for a long time, nobody gets back into it.

THE HOLIDAYS OF BED

Are when no one is there.

GEORGICS IN BED

Planting wheat and rye and oats—explaining how to do it
And when, what kind of sunlight is needed and how much rain.

STRANGE BEDFELLOWS

The bear got into bed
With his claws.

CHAIRMAN BED

There is a little red book
In the bed.

SHOWER BED

For her engagement they gave her a shower
And for her marriage they went to bed.

MANTEQUILLA BED

Butter bed, beurre bed, burro bed.

THESMOPHORIAZUSAE IN BED

Euripides put the Thesmophoriazusae in bed;
Then he also put in bed Elektra, Jason, and Sophocles.
Aristophanes said, Here, let me put you to bed.
No! Euripides screamed. But Aristophanes did
Put Euripides into bed with the Thesmophoriazusae.

POETRY BED

To have it all at once, and make no decisions.
But that is a decision.

OLIVE TREE BED

Along the side of the hill
Amid the green and gray trees
There is a place that looks like a bed.

I AM SORRY I DIDN'T EXPECT TO FIND YOU IN BED

With me I must have misdialed the telephone oh
Wait a minute—damn! I can't extricate
Myself from these sheets yes I'm getting up what
Did you expect after such a long night at the factory
Of unexplained phenomena with your head and shoulders
Beautiful as a telephone directory but please don't talk to me about love
I have an appointment with my head with the dead with a pheasant
With a song I'm nervous good-bye. It was the end of bed.

STREAM BED

In the stream bed
The snails go to sleep.

PHILOSOPHY OF BED

A man should be like a woman and a woman should be like an animal
In bed is one theory. Another is that they both should be like beds.

WE NEVER WENT TO BED

Listen, Kenny, I think it's a great idea! said Maxine
And she helped me sell my book to Chelsea House.
It was spring, with just the slightest hint of white and pink in the
  branches.

MALLARMÉ'S BED

An angel came, while Mallarmé lay in bed,
When he was a child, and opened its hands
To let white bouquets of perfumed stars snow down.

PSYCHOANALYTIC CRITICISM IN BED

What are you trying to avoid talking about
When you talk about bed?

STORM IN BED

It was such a bad storm
That we were hurled out of bed.

FLEURUS BED

There were flowers on the wallpaper,
There was loss and present excitement,
There was hope for the future, anxiety about the past,
Doubts and hopes about my work, and much to come,
As I lay in my bed on the rue de Fleurus.

CARTOON BED

The door swings open and the bed comes in
Making a tremendous racket and bumping around.

OWL IN BED

The owl flew into bed
By mistake.

DAY BED

When I loved you
Then that whole time
Was like a bed
And that whole year
Was like a day bed.

DENIED BED

We were not in bed
When summer came.

LE FORÇAT DU MOULIN À GAZ IN BED

The convict of the gas mill is in bed.

SNOW IN BED

Vanishing snowflakes, rooftops appearing
And sidewalks and people and cars as we get out of bed.

DISCOBOLUS IN BED

The discus thrower
Is still in bed.

Girl and Baby Florist Sidewalk Pram
Nineteen Seventy Something

Sweeping past the florist's came the baby and the girl
I am the girl! I am the baby!
I am the florist who is filled with mood!
I am the mood. I am the girl who is inside the baby
For it is a baby girl. I am old style of life. I am the new
Everything as well. I am the evening in which you docked your first
    kiss.
And it came to the baby. And I am the boyhood of the girl
Which she never has. I am the florist's unknown baby
He hasn't had one yet. The florist is in a whirl
So much excitement, section, outside his shop
Or hers. Who is he? Where goes the baby? She
Is immensely going to grow up. How much
Does this rent for? It's more than a penny. It's more
Than a million cents. My dear, it is life itself. Roses?
Chrysanthemums? If you can't buy them I'll give
Them for nothing. Oh no, I can't.
Maybe my baby is allergic to their spores.
So then the girl and her baby go away. Florist stands whistling
Neither inside nor outside thinking about the mountains of Peru.

With Janice

The leaves were already on the trees, the fruit blossoms
White and not ruined and pink and not ruined and we
Were riding in a boat over the water in which there was a sea
Hiding the meanings of all our salty words. A duck
Or a goose and a boat and a stone and a stone cliff. The
Hardnesses—and, with a little smile—of life. Sitting
Earlier or later and forgotten the words and the bees
At supper they were about in how you almost gestured but stopped
Knowing there were only one or two things, and that the rest
Were merely complications. But one in a trenchcoat said
It's reversible. And, It's as out-of-date as a reversible coat. And
Magna Bear and Minor Orse were sleeping. The soap
Was climbing in its dish but relaxed and came down when cold water
    stopped
Rushing in and the bathroom was flooded. I said, It is not about
Things but with things I'd like to go and, too, Will it last
Or will all become uniform again? Even as she goes
Pottering around the island's peripheries she thinks
Of the obligations. And the sympathies, far stronger than bears.
I was a bush there, a hat on a clothes dummy's head. Receiving letters
Sat down. I avoided being punished. I said,
It's cutting the limbs off a tree but there was no
Tree and I had no saw. I was planning to have infinite egress
While keeping some factory on the surface exceedingly cold. It was
A good source of evening. Sweating, asleep in the after-
Noons, later the morning of thumps, unwhittled questions, the freezing
    head. At night
Drinking whiskey, the fishermen were, everyone said, away.
A chrysanthemum though still full of splashes it
Has lost some little of its odor for my nostrils and a girl
In a chalk-pink-and-white dress is handing on the cliff
A glass of emerald water to a pin, or is it a chicken, as you get
Closer you can see it is a mirror made of the brawn
Of water muscles splashing that which has been.
My self, like the connections of an engine—rabbits and the new year—
Having puzzled out something in common, a blue stone duck
As if Homer Hesiod and Shakespeare had never lived at all

And we weren't the deposit. Weinstein puts on his hat
And the women go crazy. Some falter toward the sea. Wein-
Stein come back! But he is leaving. He says Leonard! Good-bye!
So Leonard invites us
To come and to see, where the white water bucket is a dashboard
Of this place to that. You will want to go swimming, and you will
    want to meet
These snobbish absurd Americans who inhabit
The gesso incalcations on the cliff. And we went like a nose
To a neighbor face. Sometimes tilting the grappa
Or in this case the ouzo it spills on my clothes or on yours, the world
    without us, the world outside
As when one of us was sick, which also brought the out world in.
And the art world meanwhile
Was strumming along. Individual struggles
Will long be remembered, of XXX's doing this,
Of YYYY's doing that.
Soap which will start lazily up from those types. Then
We remember to leave and also to stay. Janice said
It may not be hooked on right. Weinstein has been walking
Down a flowery way. Good-bye, nature lovers! he crescendoed.
A locked sail. The bullet of this button isn't right. And the train laughed
And pulled out pulling half of the station with it. The dust
Was indifferent to Americans as to Greeks. What simply was happening
Was beyond the rustication of ideas into the elements but essentially the
    same. Meanwhile, grasses matted,
The leaves winced, ideas one had had in earliest childhood days
Were surprisingly becoming succinct, maybe just before vanishing
Or turning into something you would feel like a belt,
Circling but not in hand. I would find these and set them down
On the sizzling white paper that was slipperier than the knees
That made me feel guilty, and sometimes heavier than the overcoats
    which there we never had
For someone's chest's attention. It was always distraction
But it was also a chair. And a chair is merely a civilized distraction. If
Character wasn't everything, it was something else I didn't
Know less than geography, which is to say, Surprise, Wonder,

Delight. You stood there and the stones
Of Old Greece and our lives, those collegiate stones,
Harvard, Emory, and Marymount, with the blue exegesis of the tide
Against which to fall was a headline—Don't stand.
You give this wish to me—Apollo, in some manner of time, lives on.
    Inside your mind
Things are being washed. Everything was docking
And we went down to see it. Memories of women made exactly the
    same
Kneeling down in the hot raft of daisies
It also got ragged for my walks. When are we going
To really have the time to have time? I make love to you
Like a rope swinging across a stone wall and you
Are lilacs reflected in a mirror or seen through a window.
Going out. You said I like this one. A pale pink dress
The suds were driving through the water. Moving fairly fast against the
Just plain oxygen we ended up looking
A little bit overcome. But I got up
You got up. We went around
Spilling things and putting a few of them on racks.
Those were the important things we never got done
Because they were behind us or
Surpassing us, otherwise unavailable—cherry
Blossoms, clavicles of girls which I can't touch
In the innocuousness, beetles, burring and scampering around a rose
I see is no longer there. Blossoms on the walk we were here, were there
As much as the heat was. I dried my ear at the sink
Then dried the other and quieted my lips and my nose
With a briny dry towel and you slid upon your shoes
And Katherine jumped up, ran around. Soon she will be
Out as usual, down the roadway formally unopened
For my approach, as if not to be drunk
Were a confidence vote from the leaves for the turmoil inside
The ouzo-fed engines of ourselves, when, seated on slabs of wood
As roses on tough ground as eggs were on the morning, deciding to
    leave,
We oversleep the boat, a shirt, a white shirt gleaming

On the photographic exception of the tide. An airlane of styles.
If it was said, It's hopeless
And you said, The gardens are going over
The edge of the overside sidewalk. Well,
Maybe and maybe not. A foot, I thought (not very intelligently)
In a shoe of newspapers, even ice unstacked about by process—
I loved the texture of your talk, and another woman's
Breast had a texture of a late summer day, while your
Eyes were walking both inside your head and in me, in each of my
    activities
While you both found the cat and he was seated, alive,
Beyond ants, on some anthill pebbles and or gravel. The bar wasn't
    closed
Or open, it was daylight-surprised. Plate glass was nowhere around.
I looked up. I put on my glasses. There were all these artists
Hot with the prayers of nineteen sixty-one—
Let us be potters, or skunks, but not
Business men! I sat down on a stone
And looked around, my last chance
To never be a doctor, as if it meant something, and a father of four—
In these minutes, of fatal decisions. Decisions! Fatal! Lazy,
Air comes in. What could it have been
To be so exciting? And the Scotch tape jumped into the air
With Leonardo out in a boat, and, miles later, acropoles of bones the
    dead
Dinosaurs and cities, tied to subjects
All of us present have forgotten—women, failing the Weinstein
Of the season. Rather inform
P.M. while you are re-estimating buttons'
Life by leaving them long-ungone-for in the midst
Of the very short walks we take down the long
Bite narrow street—At night electricity is kissing
The emasculated stars—The new things we had done, in pencil at the
    side of the napkin.
It was hot. Ce qui veut dire we, a cat sitting
On a balcony a plant was wilting. What dialect are you speaking,
You, wearing the loafers of the sea? I couldn't care

For everything simultaneously. A mat was exciting enough. The bath
  came separately
From the dawn. You walk around
Simply looking for strawberries, sun, our baby, oxygen—
"Always not quite unbeginning to be or have been begun."
Leonardo erat other. Iras haec perturbat. Let that be. Another was
Absent in a habit fidget. I was
In a rush. Someone said, hush!
Calm down in this—knife—patterns of things—
Where is the music that's fitting for such an occasion
In those miles of hotel
Corridor followed by Weinstein's weeping at the beach
Girls who followed that for love of him
And why is there not more peaceful melting here
Into the wide wood story of the wall
How I loved those made of stone. And yet poetry has
Messages, interrogations of musics that have been used
In the various islands of acts, staying genuinely still,
And seeing—a piece of life and seeing—
It's a wall inside me
Why dancers were always coming out in a pageant
Wrecking the place animals were in there too
As now, so for music fit?
The pink spot you trotted me out to see with under the sigh which
Something and the great writers were all still alive
Much of the worst had happened, the envelope was still unpeeled.
I am stamping on the path. Alone. Nothing is so essential as this—
Moment. And a red fan wings past—flower? Transatlantic systems
  ourselves
The door unopened, the mail came every day. The grass is soft,
Matted, and then there was an enclosure, tar on my leg, on yours
The culture all around us was in fragments, in some chests sure
In others fragments, in some no grasp at all, which I couldn't
Easily perceive, thus making everybody equal,
Almost at least enough to be a rival—perception,
Inspiration—too cloud to care. Voices
I heard on rooftops and cul-de-sacs of meditative sex

Scurried beyond the invisible barrier of you washing
The blouse. Brilliant. In fact, having more meaning
Because of all impulsions. You were
A blue coat—it wasn't
Exactly yours or mine or that place's
But a stinginess of life in packet flying through
Eventually, signing away like papers
A moment of the beach, when the tide dried the invincible
By elbows in comparison to the nude inside—
Look at—it's finished; this rock
Will come with me! Weinstein, walking in his sleep
The first afternoon when I arrived cooling bees they have a hive
Against the cliff, who've kept things in—the art
School, slacks. Normal the Mediterranean
Flows onward and on, boat,
I wore Leonard's jacket and my clothes, then shoes
Meet yours, advancing, so walk about the best
Final of beach, to not notice numbers
Except when they are speaking, as we stopped less
When all this was around.

Days and Nights

I. THE INVENTION OF POETRY

It came to me that all this time
There had been no real poetry and that it needed to be invented.
Some recommended discovering
What was already there. Others,
Taking a view from further up the hill (remnant
Of old poetry), said just go and start wherever you are.

It was not the kind of line
I wanted so I crossed it out
"Today I don't think I'm very inspired"—
What an existence! How hard to concentrate
On what is the best kind of existence!
What's sure is having only one existence
And its already having a shape.

Extase de mes vingt ans—
French girl with pure gold eyes
In which shine internal rhyme and new kinds of stanzas

When I said to F, Why do you write poems?
He said, Look at most of the poems
That have already been written!

All alone writing
And lacking self-confidence
And in another way filled with self-confidence
And in another way devoted to the brick wall
As a flower is when hummed on by a bee

I thought This is the one I am supposed to like best
The totally indifferent one
Who simply loves and identifies himself with something
Or someone and cares not what others think nor of time
The one who identifies himself with a wall.

I didn't think I was crazy
I thought Orpheus chasms trireme hunch coats melody
And then No that isn't good enough

I wrote poems on the edges of the thistles
Which my walking companions couldn't understand
But that's when I was a baby compared to now

"That is so much like you and your poetry."
This puts me in a self-congratulatory mood
Which I want to "feel out," so we sit together and talk
All through the winter afternoon.

I smoked
After writing five or ten lines
To enjoy what I had already written
And to not have to write any more

I stop smoking
Until after lunch
It is morning
It is spring
The day is breaking
Ten—eleven—noon
I am not smoking
I am asleep

Sense of what primitive man is, in cave and with primitive life
Comes over me one bright morning as I lie in bed
Whoosh! to the typewriter. Lunch! And I go down.

What have I lost?
The Coleridge joke, as W would say.

William Carlos Williams I wrote
As the end word of a sestina. And *grass*

Sleepy, hog snout, breath, and *dream.*
I never finished it.

I come down the hill—cloud
I like living on a hill—head
You are so lucky to be alive—jokes
It chimes at every moment—stung

So much of it was beyond me
The winding of the national highway
The fragments of glass in the convent wall
To say nothing of the habits of the bourgeoisie
And all those pleasures, the neat coat,
The bought wine, and the enabling of the pronouncements.

For Christ's sake you're missing the whole day
Cried someone and I said Shut up
I want to sleep and what he accomplished in the hours I slept
I do not know and what I accomplished in my sleep
Was absolutely nothing.

How much is in the poet and how much in the poem?
You can't get to the one but he gives you the other.
Is he holding back? No, but his experience is like a bubble.
When he gives it to you, it breaks. Those left-over soap dots are the
    work.

Oh you've done plenty I said when he was feeling despondent
Look at X and L and M. But they don't do anything, he replied.

At the window I could see
What never could be inside me
Since I was twelve: pure being
Without desire for the other, not even for the necktie or the dog.

2. THE STONES OF TIME

The bathtub is white and full of strips
And stripes of red and blue and green and white
Where the painter has taken a bath! Now comes the poet
Wrapped in a huge white towel, with his head full of imagery.

Try being really attentive to your life
Instead of to your writing for a change once in a while
Sometimes one day one hour one minute oh I've done that
What happened? I got married and was in a good mood.

We wrote so much that we thought it couldn't be any good
Till we read it over and then thought how amazing it was!

Athena gave Popeye a Butterfinger filled with stars
Is the kind of poetry Z and I used to stuff in jars

When we took a walk he was afraid
Of the dogs who came in parade
To sniffle at the feet
Of two of the greatest poets of the age.

The stars came out
And I was still writing
My God where's dinner
Here's dinner
My wife! I love you
Do you remember in Paris
When I was thinner
And the sun came through the shutters like a knife?

I said to so many people once, "I write poetry."
They said, "Oh, so you are a poet." Or they said,
"What kind of poetry do you write? modern poetry?"
Or "My brother-in-law is a poet also."

Now if I say, "I am the poet Kenneth Koch," they say, "I think I've
   heard of you"
Or "I'm sorry but that doesn't ring a bell" or
"Would you please move out of the way? You're blocking my view
Of that enormous piece of meat that they are lowering into the Bay
Of Pigs." What? Or "What kind of poetry do you write?"

"Taste," I said to J and he said
"What else is there?" but he was looking around.

"All the same, she isn't made like that,"
Marguerite said, upon meeting Janice,
To her husband Eddie, and since
Janice was pregnant this had a clear meaning
Like the poetry of Robert Burns.

You must learn to write in form first, said the dumb poet.
After several years of that you can write in free verse.
But of course no verse is really "free," said the dumb poet.
Thank you, I said. It's been great talking to you!

Sweet are the uses of adversity
Became Sweetheart cabooses of diversity
And Sweet art cow papooses at the university
And Sea bar Calpurnia flower havens' re-noosed knees

A book came out, and then another book
Which was unlike the first,
Which was unlike the love
And the nightmares and the fisticuffs that inspired it
And the other poets, with their egos and their works,
Which I sometimes read reluctantly and sometimes with great delight
When I was writing so much myself
I wasn't afraid that what they wrote would bother me
And might even give me ideas.

I walked through the spring fountain of spring
Air fountain knowing finally that poetry was everything:
Sleep, silence, darkness, cool white air, and language.

3. THE SECRET

Flaming
They seem
To come, sometimes,
Flaming
Despite all the old
Familiar effects
And despite my knowing
That, well, really they're not flaming
And these flaming words
Are sometimes the best ones I write
And sometimes not.

The doctor told X don't write poetry
It will kill you, which is a very late example
Of the idea of the immortal killing the man
(Not since Hector or one of those people practically)
X either wrote or didn't I don't remember—
I was writing (what made me think of it)
And my heart beat so fast
I actually thought I would die.

Our idea is something we talked about, our idea
Our idea is to write poetry that is better than poetry
To be as good as or better than the best old poetry
To evade, avoid all the mistakes of bad modern poets
Our idea is to do something with language
That has never been done before
Obviously—otherwise it wouldn't be creation
We stick to it and now I am a little nostalgic
For our idea, we never speak of it any more, it's been

Absorbed into our work, and even our friendship
Is an old, rather fragile-looking thing.
Maybe poetry took the life out of both of them,
Idea and friendship.

I like the new stuff you're doing
She wrote and then she quoted some lines
And made some funny references to the poems
And he said have you forgotten how to write the other kind of poems
Or, rather, she said it I forget which
I was as inspired as I have ever been
Writing half-conscious and half-unconscious every day
After taking a walk or looking at the garden
Or making love to you (as we used to say)

Unconscious meant "grace"
It meant No matter who I am
I am greater than I am
And this is greater
And this, since I am merely the vessel of it,
May be the truth

Then I read Ariosto
I fell to my knees
And started looking for the pins
I had dropped when I decided to be unconscious
I wanted to fasten everything together
As he did and make an enormous poetry Rose
Which included everything
And which couldn't be composed by the "unconscious"
(At least not by the "unconscious" alone)

This rose became a bandanna, which became a house
Which became infused with all passion, which became a hideaway
Which became yes I would like to have dinner, which became hands
Which became lands, shores, beaches, natives on the stones
Staring and wild beasts in the trees, chasing the hats of

Lost hunters, and all this deserves a tone
That I try to give it by writing as fast as I can
And as steadily, pausing only to eat, sleep, and as we used to say, make
   love
And take long walks, where I would sometimes encounter a sheep
Which gave me rhyming material and often a flowering fruit tree,
Pear apple cherry blossom thing and see long paths winding
Up hills and then down to somewhere invisible again
Which I would imagine was a town, in which another scene of the
   poem could take place.

4. OUT AND IN

City of eternal flowers
And A said Why not make it paternal flowers
And Z said Or sempiternal There were bananas
Lying on the closet shelf by the couch
Forty feet from where your miscarriage began
And we were talking about this nonsense
Which meant so much to us, meant so much to us at the time.

Ponte Vecchio going over the Arno
What an image you are this morning
In the eye of almighty God!
I am the old bridge he said she said
I forget if it was a boy or a girl
A sexless thing in my life
Like sidewalks couches and lunch

Walking around nervously then going in the house
The entire problem is to sit down
And start writing. Solved! Now the problem
Is to get up. Solved! Now the problem
Is to find something equally worthwhile to do. Solved!
Thank you for coming to see me. But
Thank you for living with me. And

Thank you for marrying me. While
Thank you for the arguments and the fights
And the deadly interpellations about the meanings of things!

Your blue eyes are filled with storms
To alter and mildly disarrange an image of someone's, he said it about
   the eyelid
But you are crying. I have a pain in my side.

The idea of Mallarmé
That
Well that it was so
Vital
Poetry, whatever it was
Is inspiring
Is I find even more inspiring
Than his more famous idea
Of absence
And his famous idea
Of an uncertain relationship of the words
In a line to make it memorably *fugace.*

Absence and I were often in my room
Composing. When I came out you and absence were wielding a broom
Which was a task I hadn't thought of in my absence
Finally absence took over
You, me, the broom, my writing, my typewriter,
Florence, the house, Katherine, everything.

Well, I don't know—those were great moments
Sometimes and terrible moments sometimes
And sometimes we went to the opera
And sometime later the automobile squeaked
There is no such thing as an automobile, there is only a Mercedes or a
   Ferrari
Or a Renault Deux Chevaux is that a Citroën
There is What do we care what kind of car but

Often in the sunshine we did. That's
When we were traveling I wasn't writing.

You've got to sit down and write. Solved!
But what I write isn't any good. Unsolved!
Try harder. Solved! No results. Unsolved!
Try taking a walk. Solved! An intelligent, pliable,
Luminous, spurting, quiet, delicate, amiable, slender line
Like someone who really loves me
For one second. What a life! (Solved!) Temporarily.

What do you think I should do
With all these old poems
That I am never going to even look at again
Or think about or revise—Throw them out!
But if I raise my hand to do this I feel like Abraham!
And no sheep's around there to prevent me.
So I take another look.

We asked the bad poet to come and dine
The bad poet said he didn't have time
The good poet came and acted stupid
He went to sleep on the couch
But grandiose inspiration had arrived for him with the wine
Such was the occasion.

Long afternoons, when I'm not too nervous
Or driven, I sit
And talk to the source of my happiness a little bit
Then Baby gets dressed but not in very much it's
Warm out and off we go
For twenty minutes or so and then come back.

Everyone in the neighboring houses
And in the neighboring orchards and fields
Is busily engaged in doing something
(So I imagine) as I sit here and write.

A B C D F I J
L M N R Y and Z were the friends I had who wrote poetry
Now A B and C are dead, L N and Y have stopped writing
Z has gotten better than ever and I am in a heavy mood
Wondering how much life and how much writing there should be—
For me, have the two become mostly the same?
Mostly! Thank God only mostly! Last night with you
I felt by that shaken and uplifted
In a way that no writing could ever do.
The body after all is a mountain and words are a mist—
I love the mist. Heaven help me, I also love you.

When the life leaves the body life will still be in the words
But that will be a little and funny kind of life
Not including you on my lap
And looking at me then shading your beautiful eyes.

Do you want me to keep telling
You things about your
Poem or do you want me to stop? Oh
Tell me. What? I don't think
You should have that phrase "burn up" in the first line.
Why not? I don't know. It
Seems a little unlike the rest.

O wonderful silence of animals
It's among you that I best perhaps could write!
Yet one needs readers. Also other people to talk to
To be friends with and to love. To go about with. And
This takes time. And people make noise,
Talking, and playing the piano, and always running around.

Night falls on my desk. It's an unusual situation.
Usually I have stopped work by now. But this time I'm in the midst of
    a thrilling evasion,

234

Something I promised I wouldn't do—sneaking in a short poem
In the midst of my long one. Meanwhile you're patient, and the veal's
    cold.

Fresh spring evening breezes over the plates
We finish eating from and then go out.
Personal life is everything personal life is nothing
Sometimes—click—one just feels isolated from personal life
Of course it's not public life I'm comparing it to, that's nonsense
    vanity—
So what's personal life? the old mom-dad-replay joke or
Sex electricity's unlasting phenomenon? That's right. And on
This spring evening it seems sensational. Long may it be lasting!

It helps me to be writing it helps me to breathe
It helps me to say anything it gives me
I'm afraid more than I give it

I certainly have lost something
My writing makes me aware of it
It isn't life and it isn't youth
I'm still young enough and alive
It's what I wrote in my poems
That I've lost, the way Katherine would walk
As far as the tree line, and how the fruit tree blossoms
Would seem to poke their way into the window
Although they were a long way outside

Yes sex is a great thing I admire it
Sex is like poetry it makes you aware of hands feet arms and legs
And your beating heart
I have never been inspired by sex, always by love
And so we talk about "sex" while thinking a little about poetry

There are very few poems
Compared to all the thought
And the activity and the sleeping and the falling in love

235

And out of love and the friendships
And all the talk and the doubts and the excitement
And the reputations and the philosophies
And the opinions about everything and the sensitivity
And the being alone a lot and having to be with others
A lot and the going to bed a lot and getting up a lot and seeing
Things all the time in relation to poetry
And so on and thinking about oneself
In this somewhat peculiar way

Well, producing a lot, that's not what
Being a poet is about, said N.
But trying to do so is certainly one of the somethings
It is about, though the products I must say are most numinous—
Wisps of smoke! while novels and paintings clouds go belching over the
    way!

Poetry, however, lives forever.
Words—how strange. It must be that in language
There is less competition
Than there is in regular life, where there are always
Beautiful persons being born and growing to adulthood
And ready to love. If great poems were as easy to create as people—
I mean if the capacity to do so were as widespread—
Since there's nothing easy about going through a pregnancy—
I suppose we could just forget about immortality. Maybe we can!

Z said It isn't poetry
And R said It's the greatest thing I ever read
And Y said I'm sick. I want to get up
Out of bed. Then we can talk about poetry
And L said There is some wine
With lunch, if you want some
And N (the bad poet) said
Listen to this. And J said I'm tired and
M said Why don't you go to sleep. We laughed
And the afternoon-evening ended
At the house in bella Firenze.

Index of Titles

239

About the Author

Kenneth Koch's books of poetry include *Days and Nights, The Burning Mystery of Anna in 1951, The Duplications, The Art of Love, The Pleasures of Peace, Thank You and Other Poems* and *Ko, or A Season on Earth.* He is also the author of a book of plays, *A Change of Hearts*; a novel, *The Red Robins*; and four books on education—*Wishes, Lies, and Dreams*; *Rose, Where Did You Get That Red?*; *I Never Told Anybody*; and *Sleeping on the Wing* (with Kate Farrell). He lives in New York City and is Professor of English at Columbia University.